Pornography

Editor: Danielle Lobban

Volume 431

independence
educational publishers

First published by Independence Educational Publishers

The Studio, High Green

Great Shelford

Cambridge CB22 5EG

England

© Independence 2023

ISBN-13: 978 1 86168 891 0

Printed in Great Britain

Zenith Print Group

Acknowledgements

The publisher is grateful for permission to reproduce the material in this book. While every care has been taken to trace and acknowledge copyright, the publisher tenders its apology for any accidental infringement or where copyright has proved untraceable. The publisher would be pleased to come to a suitable arrangement in any such case with the rightful owner.

The material reproduced in **issues** books is provided as an educational resource only. The views, opinions and information contained within reprinted material in **issues** books do not necessarily represent those of Independence Educational Publishers and its employees.

Images

Cover image courtesy of iStock. All other images courtesy of Freepik, Pixabay and Unsplash.

Additional acknowledgements

With thanks to the Independence team: Shelley Baldry, Tracy Biram, Klaudia Sommer and Jackie Staines.

Danielle Lobban

Cambridge, September 2023

Contents

Introduction

Pornography is Volume 431 in the **issues** series. The aim of the series is to offer current, diverse information about important issues in our world, from a UK perspective.

About Pornography

With children viewing porn from 8- or 9-years-old, which can lead to unrealistic expectations of sex, it is important that young people understand the issues around pornography. This book explores the risks of porn, including addiction, sexual exploitation and violence against women.

Our sources

Titles in the **issues** series are designed to function as educational resource books, providing a balanced overview of a specific subject.

The information in our books is comprised of facts, articles and opinions from many different sources, including:

* Newspaper reports and opinion pieces
* Website factsheets
* Magazine and journal articles
* Statistics and surveys
* Government reports
* Literature from special interest groups.

A note on critical evaluation

Because the information reprinted here is from a number of different sources, readers should bear in mind the origin of the text and whether the source is likely to have a particular bias when presenting information (or when conducting their research). It is hoped that, as you read about the many aspects of the issues explored in this book, you will critically evaluate the information presented.

It is important that you decide whether you are being presented with facts or opinions. Does the writer give a biased or unbiased report? If an opinion is being expressed, do you agree with the writer? Is there potential bias to the 'facts' or statistics behind an article?

Activities

Throughout this book, you will find a selection of assignments and activities designed to help you engage with the articles you have been reading and to explore your own opinions. Some tasks will take longer than others and there is a mixture of design, writing and research-based activities that you can complete alone or in a group.

Further research

At the end of each article we have listed its source and a website that you can visit if you would like to conduct your own research. Please remember to critically evaluate any sources that you consult and consider whether the information you are viewing is accurate and unbiased.

Issues Online

The **issues** series of books is complemented by our online resource, issuesonline.co.uk

On the Issues Online website you will find a wealth of information, covering over 70 topics, to support the PSHE and RSE curriculum.

Why Issues Online?

Researching a topic? Issues Online is the best place to start for...

Librarians

Issues Online is an essential tool for librarians: feel confident you are signposting safe, reliable, user-friendly online resources to students and teaching staff alike. We provide multi-user concurrent access, so no waiting around for another student to finish with a resource. Issues Online also provides FREE downloadable posters for your shelf/wall/table displays.

Teachers

Issues Online is an ideal resource for lesson planning, inspiring lively debate in class and setting lessons and homework tasks.

Our accessible, engaging content helps deepen students' knowledge, promotes critical thinking and develops independent learning skills.

Issues Online saves precious preparation time. We wade through the wealth of material on the internet to filter the best quality, most relevant and up-to-date information you need to start exploring a topic.

Our carefully selected, balanced content presents an overview and insight into each topic from a variety of sources and viewpoints.

Students

Issues Online is designed to support your studies in a broad range of topics, particularly social issues relevant to young people today.

Thousands of articles, statistics and infographs instantly available to help you with research and assignments.

With 24/7 access using the powerful Algolia search system, you can find relevant information quickly, easily and safely anytime from your laptop, tablet or smartphone, in class or at home.

Visit issuesonline.co.uk to find out more!

Chapter 1

What is Porn?

Important things to know about porn

Porn has been around for thousands of years. It's natural to be curious about sex and porn but it's also completely normal to not be interested or enjoy porn at all. Whether you do or don't watch porn, there are some things worth knowing about it.

What is porn?

Pornography, or 'porn' for short, refers to explicit images or videos that show sexual activity or sexual images in a way that is designed to make the viewer sexually excited or 'turned on'.

Porn has been around for thousands of years, beginning as images of naked people or people engaging in sexual activity carved into cave walls or painted on ancient pottery.

Being interested in sex and wanting to explore it is natural, so you shouldn't feel ashamed for wanting to watch porn. But as the internet has made porn more accessible, you may also find you come across it by accident. So, whether you watch porn or have no interest in it at all, it's worth understanding a bit more.

Why do people watch porn?

It's important to remember that everyone's porn use and likes are different. Some people watch lots of porn, others never watch it. Even among those that do watch porn, the type of porn they like can be really different.

To get turned on

The main reason some people watch porn is to get aroused (turned on), whether that's by themselves while masturbating or with a partner(s).

People may also watch porn to:

- Learn more about a particular sexual act they've heard or read about

- Discover new things about sex and sexuality

- Show off or have a laugh with friends

By accident

With so much porn out there it's possible that you may come across it by accident. You might be searching for factual information about sex, or for something completely unrelated to sex, and a video or image pops up that you weren't expecting.

> **61% of 11-13 year olds describe their viewing of porn as mostly unintentional**

> **What if I come across porn by accident?**
>
> If you see porn by accident, you should close the browser, especially if it makes you feel uncomfortable. You might be confused, worried or upset about what you've seen. Talking to a trusted adult that you feel comfortable with can help and give you the chance to ask any questions you might have.

Pressure from others

Not everyone likes porn, despite what you might think! And not wanting to watch porn is completely normal.

There are lots of reasons people don't watch porn. Some people will choose not to watch porn for religious, social, or cultural reasons while for others it might simply be that porn doesn't do anything for them. Some people prefer other ways of becoming aroused or prefer different types of porn. There are also lots of people that don't get aroused (turned on) or don't want to get aroused. For example, people who are asexual or 'aces' can feel less of a desire to have sex. You should never feel any pressure to watch porn or to enjoy it.

What porn do people watch?

Free porn websites often have lots of categories to choose from you might find that you like different types of porn to what you like in real life when you're with a sexual partner(s).

For example, you may be heterosexual (straight) but enjoy watching LGBT+ porn, or vice versa. Or you may enjoy watching certain sexual acts but wouldn't want to try them yourself.

It is normal to enjoy things in porn that you wouldn't when you have sex – your porn use and likes don't define your sexuality!

Fetishes and kinks

There are also often categories based on specific things that turn some people on, also known as fetishes and kinks. Although it's often not spoken about, having a fetish or kink isn't necessarily problematic – we're all different and enjoy different things when it comes to sex. However, some fetishes or kinks can be harmful. For example, appearance (race, hair colour, body type) and sexuality are often fetishised in porn (made into objects of sexual pleasure and arousal). This can create stereotypes and have real world consequences on how we view, respect and treat other people. Some fetishes and kinks are not socially acceptable and sometimes wouldn't be legal if you were to actually do them. There are also things that are illegal in porn and that should never be shown.

What's missing from porn?

Porn is created for entertainment – the people in it are actors and it's scripted and planned beforehand. This means that sex in porn is often not true to life.

You should treat sex in porn as just a story or fantasy that may be very different to how you or others would like to have sex.

Porn often doesn't show:

Consent

Each time you try something new you should give and get consent. Porn doesn't always show each person agreeing to sex (or different activities) beforehand, so it might seem that they've not had a conversation about it. This isn't true: people acting in porn will have agreed exactly what they will and won't do in advance.

Porn may also sometimes show people being 'persuaded' into sex, or different types of sex. But remember that they are actors acting out a scene. You should never pressure someone into sex or try to persuade them to do something if they don't want as this isn't consent.

Types of sex

There are lots of ways to have sex that don't feature as often as penetrative (penis in vagina) sex in porn. There are also certain things that are common in porn but these should never be expected when you have sex with someone:

45% of porn videos show physical aggression such as gagging, choking or slapping, usually towards women

Anal sex is also often common in porn. Occasionally, people might like type of sex but before you try anything, you need to know if your sexual partner(s) enjoys this and if they do, if this is what they want at that time. There are certain things porn ignores about anal sex which are important to understand if you do want to try this.

Condoms and safe sex

You rarely see condoms in porn videos and often see the 'pull-out method' (withdrawal) being used. It may seem like the actors in porn are using the 'pull-out method' as contraception but this isn't the case as it's not an effective way of preventing pregnancy. Instead, they use different contraception methods that aren't visible and they also test regularly for stis to make sure they're having safe sex. Whether you're using a different contraception method or if you're not having sex that could end in pregnancy, you still need to use condoms to protect against stis.

Other things missing from porn

Real orgasms

Orgasms can be faked, particularly in porn where the pleasure of the woman/person with vagina often features less than the pleasure of the man/person with a penis. Contrary to what porn might show, only 20% of people with vaginas can orgasm from penetrative (penis in vagina sex) alone, most need clitoral stimulation. It's also quite rare for two people to have an orgasm at the same time.

Representative body types

The people in porn often don't look like most of us. For example, their penis, body hair, or labia might not look like yours. The people in porn may have more muscles or bigger boobs or smaller waists than you but this isn't an accurate representation of what most people look like and many of these actors have had cosmetic surgery.

Arousal

The time it takes to become aroused (turned on) is often downplayed in porn and this build up should in itself be enjoyable.

Lube

You might not see the actors in porn reaching for the lube bottle during sex but that doesn't mean they don't use it!

Lube can make penetrative sex more enjoyable by making things more slippery.

Breaks

Porn videos are often edited to make it look like sex goes on for a long time without breaks or multiple sessions. But this isn't the reality!

Awkwardness

Sex in porn is planned and scripted to make it appealing and easy to watch. Sex in real life is a lot less smooth and can be clumsy and awkward. There's often a lot of fumbling, laughter, talking, breaks, body noises. These are all completely normal, whether it's your first time or hundredth time!

When does porn become unhealthy?

Watching porn and having an interest in sex is natural and healthy. However, because porn is so accessible and there are so many different types, it can become unhealthy and have an impact on your self-esteem, relationships, sex life and wellbeing.

Am I watching too much porn?

Porn use is different for each person. Some people don't watch it at all, other people might watch more or less than you. It's less important to focus on the amount or number of times you're watching it and more on how it's affecting your life and how you feel about it.

Questions to ask yourself:

- Are you comparing your body and sexual performance to the people in porn?
- Are you struggling to become aroused or enjoy intimacy with a sexual partner(s)?
- Are you seeking more and more extreme porn to turn you on?
- Are you copying things you've seen in porn without talking with your sexual partner(s) beforehand and during?

- Are you watching porn that disgusts you or goes against what you think is morally right?
- Are you experiencing feelings of anxiety or shame?
- Is it beginning to take over your thoughts or impacting the time you spend doing other things such as work, hobbies or socialising?
- Is it affecting your expectations of sex with your sexual partner(s)?

If you answered yes to any of these it might be that you need to get help or limit your porn use.

How can I avoid porn use becoming unhealthy?

If you're worried about your porn use or want to make sure you use porn in a safe, healthy and age-appropriate way, here are some things to consider:

- Talk to your friends and sexual partner(s) about porn
- Avoid extreme porn – if you find yourself seeking more and more extreme porn to turn you on, it might be time to take a step back
- If you usually masturbate with porn, try masturbating without it
- If you think your porn use is starting to impact your life you could set up internet controls on your phone or computer to limit your access to it

If you're over 18 you can buy ethical porn. Which is porn that is:

- Produced legally
- Provides safe working conditions for performers
- Respects and celebrates diversity
- Made with a female perspective and pleasure in mind
- Shows different types of sex

Get help

If porn is something that worries you, makes you feel bad about yourself or is harming others, it can be a really positive and important step to reach out for help and support, even if you've seen something illegal – the law is designed to protect and help young people, not to get them into trouble.

If you feel comfortable talking to an adult you know about it and how it's affecting you, that's great. You can also go to different places and organisations for support including:

- Brook or another sexual health service
- Childline
- The Mix

The above information is reprinted with kind permission from Brook.
© 2023 Brook Young People

www.brook.org.uk

A guide to pornography laws in the UK

The UK government has put extensive protections in place to ensure that the general public – particularly those under the age of 18 years old – are not adversely affected by pornography. The protections form part of a wider government effort to censor certain harmful information and materials on the Internet and elsewhere, such as copyright violations, libellous communications, depiction of animal abuse, terroristic propaganda and literature, and other extreme text, images, videos, and audio files. The purpose of this guide from our expert criminal defence solicitors is to give you an overview of some of the main laws relating to one such potentially harmful material: pornography.

Is porn illegal in the UK?

Figuring out what porn is illegal in the UK is not always a straightforward task. The regulation of pornography in the UK falls under a variety or laws, regulations, judicial processes, and even voluntary schemes. As such, there is a rarely a black and white answer to whether something is illegal. Rather, complaints about any particular material tend to have to be reviewed by regulators or judicial bodies (i.e. the courts) in order to determine its legality.

That said, the law does provide some clear-cut categories of pornographic material that is illegal in the UK. The core categories are child pornography and 'extreme pornography'. The law against child pornography in the UK is, rightly, very strict and, helpfully, relatively straightforward.

The Protection of Children Act 1978 (and its subsequent amendments) makes it illegal to take, permit to be taken, make, distribute, show, have in one's possession, publish or cause to be published any indecent photograph or pseudo-photograph of a child (defined as someone under the age of 18 years old). The law is defined broadly to allow the criminal justice system to capture a wide variety of acts that represent child pornography. The punishments for child pornography are some of the most severe of this category of offence, with up to ten years' imprisonment given to the worst offenders.

More complicated, in some ways, is the definition of 'extreme pornography', which is only a relatively recent addition to the law having come into effect in 2009.

What is 'extreme pornography'?

Government restrictions on 'extreme pornography' came about both to protect the general public from the harmful effects of such pornography, but also to protect those who are involved in the making of such materials (even if they consented to being a part of it).

The Criminal Justice and Immigration Act 2008 criminalised the possession of an 'extreme pornographic image'. According to the Crown Prosecution Service (CPS), the agency responsible for prosecuting those who are in violation of this law, an 'extreme pornographic image' is an image that is:

- Pornographic (*'of such a nature that it must reasonably be assumed to have been produced solely or principally for the purpose of sexual arousal'*), and

- Grossly offensive, disgusting or otherwise of an obscene character, and

- Portrays in an explicit and realistic way any of the following:

- An act which threatens a person's life, or

- An act which results, or is likely to result, in serious injury to a person's anus, breasts or genitals, or

- An act which involves sexual interference with a human corpse (necrophilia), or

- A person performing an act of intercourse or oral sex with an animal (whether dead or alive) (bestiality), or

- An act which involves the non-consensual penetration of a person's vagina, anus or mouth by another with the other person's penis or part of the other person's body or anything else (rape or assault by penetration) and a reasonable person looking at the image would think that the persons or animals were real.

In any criminal case involving extreme pornographic images, it will fall to the judge or jury to determine whether an image should be accordingly classified. Importantly, the intention of the defendant is not to be considered relevant to the proceedings, which means that even if someone claims not to have fully understood what the image contained or otherwise made an excuse about their intentions in possessing the image, it would make no difference to the outcome of the case.

Unlike child pornography cases, where there are several grades to the offence depending on one's involvement in the illegal activity, with extreme pornography there is only the offence of 'possession'. This is, however, a broad definition, so even those who might limit their involvement to publishing or distributing the material could readily be charged with possession.

What are the sentences for extreme pornography?

Punishments for being found guilty of possession of extreme pornography vary, but the maximum penalty is two years' imprisonment and/or a fine for cases involving necrophilia or bestiality. For other images, the maximum is three years' imprisonment and/or a fine.

If the offender is over the age of 18 years old and has been given a sentence longer than two years imprisonment, there may also be notification requirements appended to the sentence under the Sexual Offences Act 2003. This means that in certain circumstances, the offender must notify the police:

- of any and all foreign travel, even for a day

- where they are on a weekly basis (if not able to provide details of a sole residential address where he or she might be found)

- where they are living if there is a child (someone under the age of 18) also resident at that address

- of a number of personal identification and financial documents, including bank accounts, credit cards, passports, driving licences, and other documentation that shows a person's name (intended to stop people from changing their name so as not to appear on the sex offenders register)

What is the law on possessing and/or making indecent images?

Because pornography laws in the UK are so broad, sometimes people will be charged with a broader offence involving possessing and/or making indecent images rather than a specific child pornography or extreme pornography offence. Much depends on what the CPS considers to be the most appropriate charge taking into account the offender, his or her history, and any evidence to support the case.

Broadly speaking, separate offences exist for 'possession' and for 'making' indecent images (in any case, these are often prosecuted at the same time).

- 'Possessing' means the physical or digital possession of a prohibited image, which usually manifests as a file on a mobile phone or computer, printed/hard-copy materials, or a computer created/manipulated image. The offence may even be charged where a file has been deleted, as the imprint of the file still remains in the possession of the individual on their hard drive.

- 'Making' not only refers to a broad range of activities in addition to the straightforward 'making' of images, such as taking a photograph or filming a video. 'Making' can even occur when, for example, an image is downloaded, saved to an internal or external memory device, copied, shared, or sold.

With each of these offences, the intention of the person is taken into account. For some people, downloading will genuinely be an accident, either because they clicked on something they should not have (not knowing what it was) or were maliciously sent 'unknown' files by email that turned out to be indecent images.

The punishments for possessing or making indecent images vary considerably but could be up to six years' imprisonment for the most serious cases.

What was the 2019 'Porn Law' and what does it cover?

In April 2019, the Digital Economy Act 2017 (colloquially known as the 'Porn Law') came into effect across the UK. The Act covered many areas relating to electronic communications and copyright but is best known for its plans to restrict access to online pornography.

The one provision of the law that drew considerable attention was the plan to create an age verification system that would prevent people under the age of 18 years old from accessing commercially operated pornography websites. With such an age verification system in place, the law would allow regulators to fine websites up to £250,000 (or up to 5% of their turnover) and issue blocks or cease-and-desist orders to non-compliant websites.

The implementation of this age verification system proved to be contentious and ended up being one of the most heavily criticised areas of the Porn Law. Critics considered that such a system raised serious privacy concerns because of the need to collect user data, and in any case would easily be hacked or bypassed with virtual private networks (VPNs) or anonymous browsers, rendering the law useless in practice. Such extensive criticism of this aspect of the law eventually led the government to put age verification blocks on hold for the time being.

The above information is reprinted with kind permission from Stuart Miller Solicitors.
© 2023 Stuart Miller Solicitors

www.stuartmillersolicitors.co.uk

The things I wish my parents had known

An extract.

Pornography

Porn is too easily accessible online for children and they are seeing it earlier than some parents realise. Children and young people sometimes access it out of curiosity, or sometimes their viewing is accidental and unwanted. In either circumstance, viewing porn too young can be very damaging and can warp children's understanding of sex and consent and there has been a link found between porn consumption and harmful attitudes and behaviours towards women and girls.

Young people's view

Our group of young people felt porn doesn't show sex as it really is. Issues of concern include degradation and violence towards women, how consent is portrayed, and unattainable body standards.

They felt that watching porn, particularly at young ages, can affect real-life behaviours and attitudes around gender roles, sex and consent.

Girls talked about being sent porn by older boys at school. This can be scary and distressing and they would like to be able to talk to their parents about it. They also feel that parents of boys should be talking about why this kind of behaviour is not okay.

How, when and why children are viewing porn

- Over half of 11–13-year-olds have already seen pornography.

- Many children view porn unintentionally for the first time – 62% of 11–13-year-olds say that their viewing of porn was mostly or more unintentional.

- Parents' perceptions of how much porn their children are watching does not match the reality: only 25% of parents think that their child has seen porn – compared to 53% of children who have.

The legality of viewing porn

Under the current law, it is illegal for shops to sell under-18s physical copies of pornography (e.g. DVDs, videos, magazines). However there is currently a gap in the law around online pornography, which is freely available. The Children's Commissioner is working with the Government to close this loophole and bring pornography under the scope of the Online Safety Bill. In the meantime parents should be vigilant about the material their child has access to and apply parental controls where necessary.

Top tips from 16–21 year-olds

Apply adult content filters to your child and family devices. This is the best way to prevent them from stumbling across explicit content too young.

Keep it casual. Find everyday opportunities to speak about porn in an age-appropriate way. Don't allow porn to become a 'taboo' subject.

'It shouldn't be a taboo. It should be something that parents talk about to their kids.'

Be reassuring about the confusing emotions your child might feel after seeing explicit content.

Telling your child off for watching porn is not always the best response. It could make your child less likely to come to you for help/advice. Explain clearly and calmly why watching adult content too young can be harmful.

'Don't punish instead of having a proper good talk.'

Be prepared to challenge views that may arise from watching adult content. Reinforce the message that sex and bodies, as depicted in a lot of porn, are not realistic. Explain that porn can make things like non-consensual sex appear 'normal' or 'okay' but it is not.

' I feel like the best time for parents to have a conversation about porn is a bit earlier for boys than girls. From my experience of male friends, they definitely see porn earlier than my female friends. I mean like early: year 4, year 5, year 6.'

'At that young age you don't really know what's right and wrong and you just follow whatever you see on porn sites.'

'Now porn has infiltrated mainstream media, you can literally find porn on Twitter.'

– All quotes from young people aged 16–21

The above information is reprinted with kind permission from the Children's Commissioner
© 2023 Children's Commissioner for England

www.childrenscommissioner.gov.uk

Porn – how sex is sold back to us

Children are being exposed to pornography at a younger age than ever before. Isabel Ringrose explains that porn is a symptom of commodification, sexism and violence in a capitalist society.

Pornography is now increasingly common, increasingly available and increasingly normalised. Once, porn was denounced as a product of degraded liberalism. Now some celebrate it as an example of freedom and sexual openness. Neither of those reflect pornography's roots in the commodification and sexualisation of women's bodies.

It is this process that means porn portrays the worst of society's stereotypes. Women's bodies are there for the taking – to be commented on, bought, used or abused – while they have little agency over their own sex lives.

But the problem goes much deeper than porn itself. Even if we – or some state ban – removed porn from society, sexism wouldn't melt away. If only it were that easy. Everything under capitalism becomes distorted as something to be sold and bought, including our bodies and our sex lives.

And this is done in a process shaped by oppression – particularly women's oppression. Porn reflects and reinforces dominant views that exist and amplifies them to an extreme level. It paints an unnatural picture of our most intimate experiences, body image, behaviour, and how we interact with sexual partners.

Women are generally submissive, passive and always willing to please in porn. Black women and men are racialised, and gay men are reduced to stereotypes. These caricatures represent the roles set out for us in our everyday lives, and that our rulers benefit from. Porn isn't produced to teach about sex or even give us real pleasure.

In a class system where profit reigns, the ruling ideas are the dominant ones. Women's oppression is a central column to that society – reinforcing a family unit that provides for the reproduction of the next generation of workers.

Capitalism has always constrained, limited and outlawed sexuality at different times. Being gay was only partly decriminalised in Britain in 1967, the same year the pill was made legal. Marital rape was legal until 2003.

While activists, including socialists, have fought hard for sexual liberation, capitalism has managed to sell our liberation back to us. This is what commodification does – uses oppression to hold us down and then seek to profit by peddling a false version of emancipation.

Porn is one of the biggest examples of this. So are dating apps that make you pay to find what is supposed to be your 'perfect match' and whittle your personality down to a few words and pictures. Under capitalism, workers are alienated from their labour. But what does this have to do with porn?

Porn is the exemplification of that alienation. Karl Marx wrote that under capitalism, we are disconnected from this very thing that makes us human. Humans – unlike other animals – have a capacity for consciousness or a 'species being'. We are social creatures, so enter relationships in order to live and keep connected.

But under class society, and in particular capitalism, we have very little control over how our labour is used and what it produces. We are forced to work to live. And the thing that makes us unique – our labour power – is sold for a wage. As a result we are also alienated from each other and ourselves and forced to connect through buying and selling commodities.

We're told our needs can only be met through purchasing things. These needs – food, drink, sex – are subordinated to the market and reshaped, then turned into consumer dreams. Women, especially, are pushed to buy endless products to make them more beautiful, thinner, and more desirable.

The bosses try to make profits out of every sexual need. We're told we're liberated if we have 'stuff'. The best cookers, hoovers, furniture, clothes, make-up and shoes are, we're told, essential to happiness.

We do need to eat and clothe ourselves and to find joy in art and plenty. But the pushing of goods by corporations is solely about profit. And often the picture of an ideal life reinforces the subordinate role women are supposed to play in society.

We see each other as commodities to be captured or won rather than as individuals. That's why buying or watching porn as a commodity alienates and distorts our relationships. There's no room for intimacy or connection. Sex is just limited to an act.

The online porn industry is worth £20 billion worldwide. Some estimates put if far higher. It's bigger than Netflix or the whole of Hollywood streaming. By the age of 13, 50 percent of children have seen porn, with one in ten having viewed it by age nine.

It creates a particular view of sex. Some 47 percent of girls aged 16–21 'expect violence' in sex. It's marketed as escapism or 'fantasy' where anything is possible, and boundaries are pushed. Unfortunately, this so-called fantasy can quickly seep into reality.

Porn becomes real for the girl whose boyfriend strangles her or the woman cat-called in the street. It's no wonder our vision of what sex is and how it should happen is warped when all that's on offer is porn. And despite sex being

everywhere around us, the overt use of women's bodies doesn't equate to freer and better sex for everyone.

Instead, women are seen as an object. The pressure on women's bodies starts at a young age. For instance, toddlers' shorts are tighter and shorter for girls. The old phrase 'sex sells' is used to market cars, perfume and even M&M chocolates.

Women are encouraged to find a partner and please them without taking into consideration their own desires. At the same time they're condemned for having 'too much' sex as well as 'not enough'. We see reflections of how our rulers want us to live through things like porn. But it's not that leaders like Rishi Sunak spend their spare time directing porn scenes to control us.

Instead porn transmits ideas about the position of women under capitalism – a specific economic and ideological role as caregivers, mothers and child rearers.

This has shifted over time – not many women get married nowadays expecting to stay at home. Women make up just under half of the workforce globally and face the double burden of bringing in a wage as well as keeping the family running.

That's why women earn less than men, work fewer hours and have shorter careers. The family is where the next generation of workers comes from. They're raised to adulthood, ready to enter the workplace for free within the family unit. To ensure this, from day one, we're fed the myth that women are nurturing and caring – woe betide she's bossy and aggressive.

We're socialised for free in the family too. Girls play with dolls and kitchens, while boys play with tools and trains. So the expectations are set out for us way before we reach porn – even if children watch it from a younger age. Our relationships become completely distorted as we relate to each other as commodities.

And the need to please and stay passive is directly rooted in the home, the family unit, and women's place within it. Porn creates a vicious cycle where what's on the screen plays out in real life, and what's on the screen comes from society's expectations for us in the first place.

We're buying and selling our connections with each other – and basing our expectations and desires on warped versions of reality. There have been attempts to reinvent porn to make it 'ethical' or more realistic of what sex is like. And those creating independent content say this gives them more autonomy over what they do and how they do it.

But the solution shouldn't be a nicer version of something bad. There's still an exchange of money – whether between those making the content or those watching it. And even in so-called ethical porn our sexual desires which are part of what makes us human are still commodified.

It can't tackle the alienation we feel from each other and what we're watching, and the sexism ingrained in society isn't tackled at its core. In terms of real liberation, we can do better. But to achieve true sexual liberation, it will take looking deeper at the cause, not the symptom, of the sexualisation and objectification of women.

We need a wider vision of the type of society we could live in. That's a socialist one, where we truly own our bodies and sexuality – without them being reduced to on-screen acts that disconnect and distort us.

5 February 2023

'I identified with what she said': Billie Eilish remarks on porn resonate in UK

Singer's comments may help children and adults to have better conversation, say experts, amid calls to change online safety bill.

By Harriet Grant and Dan Milmo

When Billie Eilish said this week that viewing pornography at a young age had 'devastated' her, 19-year-old Jay recognised the feeling and the experience.

'I really identified with what she said. I first saw porn at about 12 or 13 on social media; it came up on Instagram and boys at school would show it around and laugh,' says Jay, who preferred not to use her real name. 'Boys talked a lot about porn, especially as we got older. It was less socially acceptable for girls to say they watched it, though we all did, I think.'

Jay, who attended a mixed comprehensive in south-west England, said pornography had 'really affected how I view my body and sex'. She added: 'It's now I'm older and I'm having sex that I am aware that I have a strong feeling of how sex should be performed and this makes me really sad. I don't know how to undo that thinking. I'm starting to feel porn actually damaged me.'

Advocates for age assurance, a range of measures to check someone's age before they access a website or app, say under-18s can access pornography too easily. A survey by the British Board of Film Classification last year found that 60% of children between 11 and 13 who reported having seen pornography said it was largely unintentional.

Speaking on the Howard Stern Show on Sirius XM radio on Monday, Eilish, who turned 20 on Saturday, said viewing porn at a young age had caused her emotional damage.

'I think porn is a disgrace. I used to watch a lot of porn, to be honest. I started watching porn when I was, like, 11,' the top-selling US singer said, adding that it helped her feel as if she were cool and 'one of the guys'.

'I think it really destroyed my brain and I feel incredibly devastated that I was exposed to so much porn,' she said, adding that she suffered nightmares because some of the content she watched was so violent and abusive. Eilish said that it had an impact on her first sexual relationships. 'The first few times I, you know, had sex, I was not saying no to things that were not good. It was because I thought that's what I was supposed to be attracted to,' she said.

Clare McGlynn, a professor of law at Durham University, said Eilish's comments could help children and adults have a 'better conversation about what material is out there on the mainstream sites'. She added: 'I think her comments will help us to have a more open conversation, because certainly young people will be able to relate to her.'

This week, a joint committee of MPs and peers recommended sweeping changes to the online safety bill, which imposes a duty of care on tech companies to protect children from harmful content. The 192-page report recommended that an updated bill requires all pornography sites to prevent children from accessing their content and called for the introduction of minimum standards for age assurance measures, from entering your date of birth on a pop-up form to more stringent age verification. Under the current terms of the bill, commercial pornography sites would not have to adhere to the legislation if they did not host user-generated content – the form of digital content that is the draft bill's focus.

McGlynn said bringing all porn publishers into the scope of the bill would be a 'very positive step forward' but legislation was only 'one part' of a solution to the problem. 'Young people are still going to find ways to access this pornography. They're still going to be looking at it, using it and thinking about it. So we still have to have the conversations with them, have a better public conversation about it and have far better sex education in schools,' she said.

Dr Fiona Vera-Gray, a colleague of McGlynn at Durham University who has researched the impact of pornography on young women, said the ease with which adult sites could be seen, and their content shared among friends, was 'frightening'. She added: 'We have abandoned a generation. They get no sex education and too much sexualised material.'

Jay says she stopped watching pornography when she was 17 but remains angry about how easy it was to access it.

'I watched it through my teen years, say 13 to 17, but then I made a choice to stop. I feel angry now at how much I saw, how easy it was to watch it.'

19 December 2021

'A lot of it is actually just abuse'– Young people and pornography

An extract.

At what age are children first exposed to pornography?

The survey found that, of the young people who said that they had ever seen online pornography, the average age at which they had first seen it was 13. There is no significant difference by gender; girls are as likely as boys to have seen pornography at this age. This is consistent with BBFC and *Revealing Reality* research, which found a majority of young people had seen pornography by age 13.

'I think when you've got a phone you've got access to it' – Boy, 16, focus group.

Young people who participated in CCo focus groups agreed that children are likely to see pornography between the ages of 11 to 12, and that this is determined by the age at which children first have their own device (smartphone, laptop or tablet). One boy shared his concern that this age is decreasing:

'I think as time goes on it is going to be younger because people seem to get devices at younger ages ... I think the age is getting younger from when we were that age' – Boy, 17, focus group.

The majority (73%) of respondents who had seen pornography had done so by age 15. Focus group participants noted that the 'novelty' of pornography wanes with age. As one boy explained:

'[Pornography] is this new exciting thing and they're showing their friends and it spreads around ... But the older you get the less you share it because everyone knows that it's there' – Boy, 17, focus group.

A significant minority of children access pornography at very young ages; 10% had seen pornography by age nine, 27% had seen it by age 11 and half (50%) of children who had seen pornography had seen it by age 13.

Young people's views on pornography

Expectations of sex

'Viewing online pornography affects young people's expectations around sex and relationships' is the statement which received the most support from participants; 72% agreed and just 4% disagreed with the statement. Girls were significantly more likely to agree than boys (76% compared to 67%).

Percentage of respondents aged 16-21 who selected each route to viewing pornography.

Includes only those who had ever viewed online pornography.

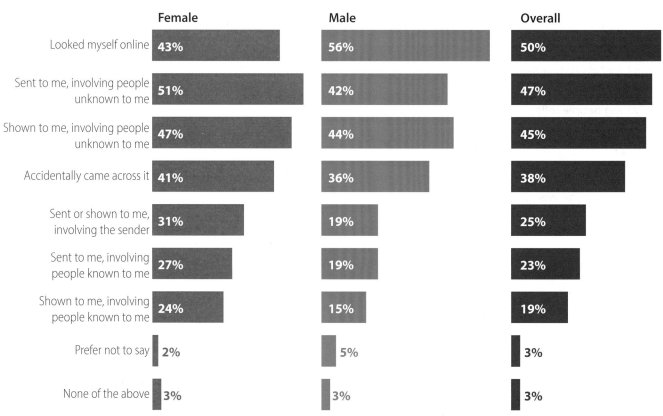

	Female	Male	Overall
Looked myself online	43%	56%	50%
Sent to me, involving people unknown to me	51%	42%	47%
Shown to me, involving people unknown to me	47%	44%	45%
Accidentally came across it	41%	36%	38%
Sent or shown to me, involving the sender	31%	19%	25%
Sent to me, involving people known to me	27%	19%	23%
Shown to me, involving people known to me	24%	15%	19%
Prefer not to say	2%	5%	3%
None of the above	3%	3%	3%

Source: The Children's Commissioner

Young people's agreement with statements related to pornography and relationships

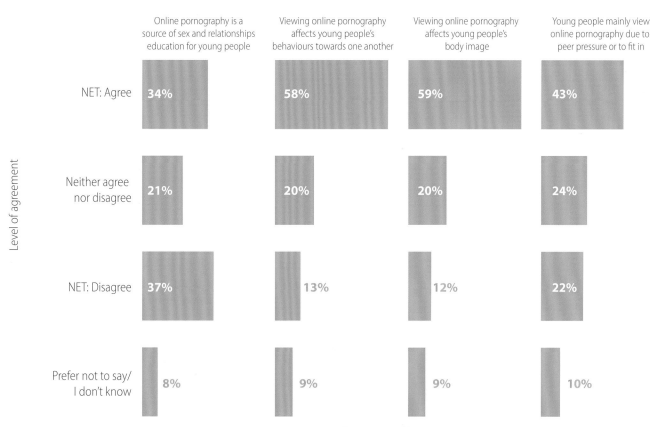

	Online pornography is a source of sex and relationships education for young people	Viewing online pornography affects young people's behaviours towards one another	Viewing online pornography affects young people's body image	Young people mainly view online pornography due to peer pressure or to fit in
NET: Agree	34%	58%	59%	43%
Neither agree nor disagree	21%	20%	20%	24%
NET: Disagree	37%	13%	12%	22%
Prefer not to say/ I don't know	8%	9%	9%	10%

Level of agreement

Percentage of responses

Source: The Children's Commissioner

All survey respondents were aged 16 and over. Many felt, themselves, able to distinguish between the artifice of pornography and the reality of real sex and relationships. The most frequently used word, across all free-text responses, was 'unrealistic'.

'A lot of online pornography can be unrealistic and some of it is rape content, so young people may think this is okay and realistic. When in reality it is not acceptable, it teaches incorrect and disgusting behaviours' – Girl, 18, survey, first saw pornography at age 12.

Some young people reflected on how their own perception of pornography had changed after they had sex:

'Younger people watch porn and don't understand that it's not real and its entirely fake … Looking back on it even I did myself. You don't realise till your older that it's not real and real sex is nothing like pornography depicts' – Boy, 21, survey, first saw pornography at age 14.

Body image

A majority of male and female respondents agreed with the statement 'viewing online pornography affects children and young people's body image' (59% agreement, 12% disagreement). Female respondents were significantly more likely than boys to agree with this statement (66% of girls agreed compared to 51% of boys).

The pressure associated with so-called 'body ideals' and the 'narrow conception of attractiveness' promoted by pornography was discussed in free-text responses and focus group discussions. Young women in the survey reflected on pornography's role in fuelling body insecurity and anxiety:

'With women's bodies not everyone has big boobs, a nice ass, a pink pussy? Like women of colour have darker nipples and stuff and men don't understand that because it's all they see. You see a lot of stuff like barely legal teens on porn sites and it's not nice. They want us to act like porn models but we can't change who we are, what we like, what we are afraid of' – Girl, 19, survey, first saw pornography at age 10.

Male respondents were also attuned to the role of pornography in informing unrealistic and unobtainable body ideals:

'It makes them think that bodies in porn are bodies in real life. People in porn are actors and they are cast based on their unrealistic bodies, during sex people will be disappointed when not everyone looks like a pornstar' – Boy, 19, survey, first saw pornography at age 10.

Young people's concerns are supported by research on the relationship between pornography consumption and body satisfaction. Several longitudinal studies show an association between adolescent pornography use and self-critical evaluation of sexual performance and body image, among both young women and young men.

'Children are being raised up to believe having a 10 inch is normal' – Boy, 21, survey, first saw pornography at age 11.

Attitudes towards women and girls

Young people also discussed the impact of pornography on perceptions of gender roles. Free-text responses highlight pornography's depiction of sex as a transactional, one-way interaction, in which women perform as objects for male gratification, as one respondent set out:

'Males can be led to believe women are purely for sex' – Boy, 18, survey, first saw pornography at 13.

It is important to acknowledge that pornography is not the only reason that harmful attitudes may develop and there are a number of reasons that a child may choose to perform a harmful sex act. However, it is clear, to young people's minds at least, that pornography plays a key role in normalising and condoning sexual violence against women.

Survey respondents discussed how sex in pornography is orientated toward male pleasure, and how this may shape regressive attitudes towards gender roles in real-life sexual relationships.

'Many heterosexual men grow up to have certain expectations of how to treat women when having sex, and in general. A lot of that is actually just abuse' – Boy, 18, survey, first saw pornography at 12.

This is at odds with young people's perceptions of healthy romantic and sexual relationships. When asked, in a focus group discussion, what constitutes a 'healthy romantic relationship', trust was the most frequent answer given by young people, followed by boundaries, consent, comfort, honesty and communication.

Each of these principles sit in stark contrast to young people's descriptions of relationships in pornography, which they characterise as impersonal, unequal and transactional.

'It reinforces negative ideas towards young people and children that women have a place below men, they are objects of desire, and can be hurt and sexually abused as long as it results in male gratification' – Non-binary, 18, survey, first saw pornography at age 7.

For this reason, young people expressed concern about the implications of pornography in distorting their understanding of the difference between sexual pleasure and harm, particularly for women.

'For example, a younger individual who is not fully developed could find pornography that reinforces abusing women and they might begin to think that is what women find pleasurable' – Girl, 21, survey, first saw pornography at age 15.

Some female respondents wrote about how pornography shaped their views on whether sex should be pleasurable for them and came, at a young age, to believe that sex should be for men's enjoyment, and not for their own.

'I was exposed to pornography at a young age and it's affected me in my adult relationships and my body image and how my sex life is currently' – Girl, 18, survey, first saw pornography at age 11.

Harmful sexual behaviour and intimate partner violence

Of perhaps greatest concern, young people discussed the influence of pornography in informing real-life sexual aggression and harmful sexual behaviour towards girls, as one boy put it:

'It can cause them to be violent and want to try it to see how it feels' – Boy, 21, survey, first saw pornography at age 15.

Most survey respondents (58%) agreed with the statement 'viewing online pornography affects young people's behaviours towards one another'. Agreement for this statement was broadly consistent across age and gender, however young people who had never seen pornography were significantly less likely to agree than the average respondent (51% agreed compared to 58%, respectively).

Young people wrote about the consequences of pornography in fuelling cultures of sexual harassment among male peer groups. Some female survey respondents shared personal experience of this, for example:

'In high school I know among boys at least they'd act like animals with it and would find the most grotesque porn they could to show their friends and get a laugh but they airdropped like this video of two guys with whole arms inside them and their prolapsing anuses flopped out and honestly that scarred me LMAO but yeah I also feel like porn might be a contributing factor to the oversexualisation of women and like the schoolgirl trope in porn led to me being sexually harassed often and it's just it affects young minds growth that's for sure' – Girl, 18, survey, first saw pornography at age 9.

Pornography can shape a person's 'sexual scripts', i.e. what they feel to be normal and legitimate in sexual situations. In turn, these influence behaviour. Given the high prevalence of sexual violence, predominantly towards women, in mainstream online pornography there is serious cause for concern about pornography's role in priming sexual behaviour among children.

'They will be more likely to interact in a pornographic manner with their peers (either sending or saving nudes, groping etc)' – Girl, 19, survey, first saw pornography at age 12.

Survey respondents wrote about the re-enactment of sexually aggressive or coercive acts seen in pornography.

'Often times porn is not just sex, but showcases a range of violent kinks like choking and spanking etc, specifically with a woman being the recipient … young children who come across porn are also more likely to try to recreate these sexual behaviours with their peers as they have been exposed to it' – Girl, 21, survey, first saw pornography at age 14.

Female respondents wrote about the pressure to perform acts which boys may have seen in pornography, including aggressive, degrading and pain-inducing sex acts. As two girls wrote in response to the survey:

'It makes boys think they can do everything they see in porn in real life. Some things like anal are everywhere in porn but most girls don't want to do that. Boys just think it's normal and expect us all to do it and it puts pressure on us' – Girl, 16, survey, first saw pornography at age 10.

'We don't want to be choked unless we consent, not everyone wants to have anal' – Girl, 19, survey, first saw pornography at age 10.

January 2023

More than one in five boys look for information about sex from porn, report finds

Report from SafeLives highlights gaps in relationships and sex education classes.

By Olivia Petter

More than one in five (22 per cent) boys are looking for information about sex through pornography, a new report has found.

According to SafeLives, a UK charity working to put an end to domestic abuse, relationships and sex education (RSE) is 'falling seriously short' of what young people need despite the curriculum receiving its first update in 20 years in 2019.

The report also found that the majority of LGBT+ students (61 per cent) disagree that LGBT+ relationships are being threaded throughout RSE.

Meanwhile, other shortages came by way of abusive relationships, with just 46 per cent of students saying they feel confident about who to talk to if they know someone who is experiencing abuse.

Additionally, only 24 per cent of those surveyed recall being taught about coercive control in RSE.

The findings were conducted via interviews, surveys and focus groups with more than 1,000 students and 60 RSE teachers in secondary schools across England.

Suzanne Jacob OBE, chief executive of SafeLives, commented: 'At SafeLives, we are passionate about stopping abuse before it starts, and education is the single most powerful preventative tool we have.

'Our team has found some glaring gaps in the delivery of this new guidance. RSE should be equipping young people, often engaging in their first intimate relationships, with the support, knowledge and confidence to navigate relationships safely and healthily.

Instead, students feel let down and that they should be getting much more out of these classes - leaving many, especially boys, looking online for answers.'

Jacobs added: 'We want to see schools across the country embedding a whole-school approach to RSE, where all members of a school community - students, staff, parents and governors - ensure RSE is prioritised and teachers are provided with the resources and time they need to build trust with their students.'

12 December 2022

Key Facts

- 22% of boys look at porn to find information about sex.

- 46% of students feel confident about who to talk to if they know someone is experiencing abuse.

Half of Britons under 30 have seen pornography while underage

In the UK, you must be 18 by law to watch pornography, and the government's latest attempt to regulate access – the Online Safety Bill – will legally require websites that publish explicit content to check that their users are over 18.

YouGov research reveals that many young Britons who have seen porn while underage, including half of Britons aged 18-29 (50%). Only 7% of this age group were aged 18 or over the first time they say they saw it, while another 13% say they have never seen pornography (the remaining 18% either could not recall their age or declined to answer).

Similarly, four in 10 Britons in their 30s (41%) first saw pornography while underage, falling to a third of Britons in their 40s (32%), a quarter of Britons in their 50s (24%) and just 10% of those aged 60 and over.

Overall, 28% of Britons watched porn for the first time underage, while 29% were over 18, and 24% have never seen porn at all.

Four in ten men (41%) first saw porn while underage, rising to 59% of 18-29 year old men. By contrast, only 17% of women have done so.

Three in 10 Britons have seen pornography underage
How old were you when you first watched pornography? %

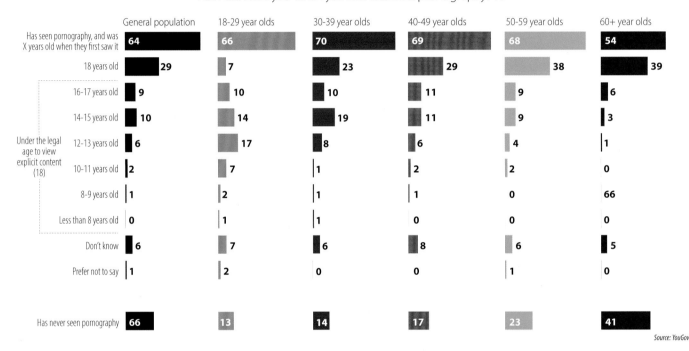

	General population	18-29 year olds	30-39 year olds	40-49 year olds	50-59 year olds	60+ year olds
Has seen pornography, and was X years old when they first saw it	64	66	70	69	68	54
18 years old	29	7	23	29	38	39
16-17 years old	9	10	10	11	9	6
14-15 years old	10	14	19	11	9	3
12-13 years old	6	17	8	6	4	1
10-11 years old	2	7	1	2	2	0
8-9 years old	1	2	1	1	0	66
Less than 8 years old	0	1	1	0	0	0
Don't know	6	7	6	8	6	5
Prefer not to say	1	2	0	0	1	0
Has never seen pornography	66	13	14	17	23	41

Under the legal age to view explicit content (18)

Source: YouGov

Six in 10 young men have seen porn underage
How old were you when you first watched pornography?
% of 4043 Britons saying they have seen pornography and were younger than 18 when they first watched it

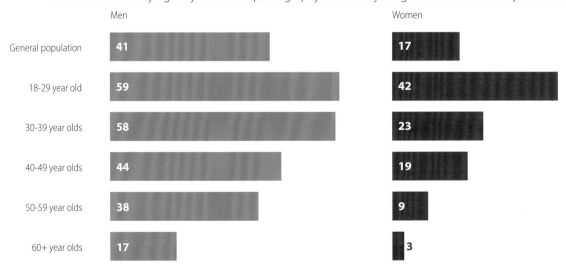

	Men	Women
General population	41	17
18-29 year old	59	42
30-39 year olds	58	23
40-49 year olds	44	19
50-59 year olds	38	9
60+ year olds	17	3

Source: YouGov

One in eight young men watched pornography when they were younger than 12 years old

How old were you when you first watched pornography? %

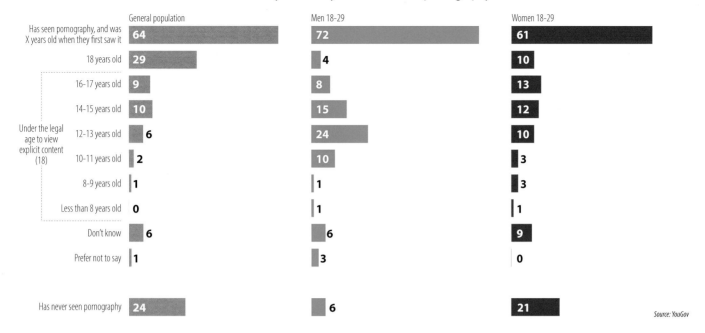

	General population	Men 18-29	Women 18-29
Has seen pornography, and was X years old when they first saw it	64	72	61
18 years old	29	4	10
16-17 years old	9	8	13
14-15 years old	10	15	12
12-13 years old	6	24	10
10-11 years old	2	10	3
8-9 years old	1	1	3
Less than 8 years old	0	1	1
Don't know	6	6	9
Prefer not to say	1	3	0
Has never seen pornography	24	6	21

Under the legal age to view explicit content (18): 16-17 years old through Less than 8 years old

Source: YouGov

Regular porn-watchers are more likely to have specifically searched for pornography the first time they saw it

Thinking about your first experience watching pornography, which statement most applies to you?
% of 2566 Britons who have ever seen pornography

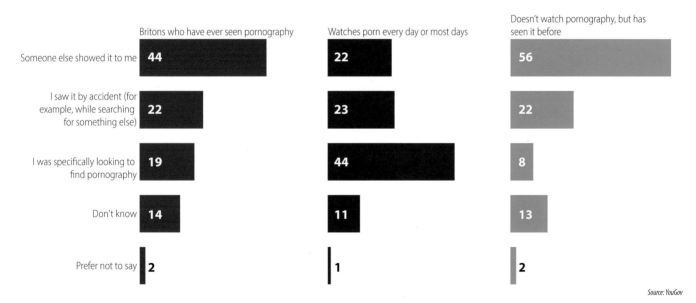

	Britons who have ever seen pornography	Watches porn every day or most days	Doesn't watch pornography, but has seen it before
Someone else showed it to me	44	22	56
I saw it by accident (for example, while searching for something else)	22	23	22
I was specifically looking to find pornography	19	44	8
Don't know	14	11	13
Prefer not to say	2	1	2

Source: YouGov

First experiences: regular porn-watchers are more likely to have specifically searched for porn the first time they saw it

Overall, more than four in 10 Britons who have seen porn say someone else showed it to them the first time they saw it (44%). A further 22% say they saw it by accident, while 19% were specifically looking to find pornography.

Regular porn-watchers are much more likely to have specifically looked for pornography the first time they saw it: more than four in 10 (44%) Britons who watch porn every day or most days say they were specifically looking to find porn when they first viewed it. A further 23% say they saw it by accident and 22% were shown explicit material by someone else.

Conversely, people who have seen porn, but don't watch it, are much more likely to say that their first experience watching porn was because someone else showed it to them (56%). Just 8% were specifically looking for pornography when they first saw it, and 22% say they saw it by accident.

1 July 2022

How prevalent is pornography?

By Daniel Cox, Beatrice Lee & Dana Popky

In the internet era, online pornography has become ubiquitous. Roughly six in 10 (58 percent) Americans report having watched pornography at some point in their lives, including more than one in four (27 percent) who have watched it in the past month. But there are massive gender differences in the consumption of pornography. Men are four times more likely than women to report having watched pornography in the past month (44 percent vs. 11 percent).

Men in their 30s and 40s report the most frequent use of pornography. A majority (57 percent) of men ages 30–49 report having watched pornography in the past month, and 42 percent say they have watched it in the past week. In contrast, 44 percent of young men and only 26 percent of senior men say they have watched pornography at some point during the past month.

Even if most Americans do not report engaging in this activity regularly, exposure to pornography is much more common today than it was in the past, particularly among women. More than eight in 10 (81 percent) women age 65 or older say they have never watched pornography, while less than half (44 percent) of young women say the same.

The Pornography Problem

The widespread availability of pornography online has made it easier to access. Most young adults say they have watched pornography at some point in their lives. But regularly watching pornography is associated with a number of negative social outcomes and personal experiences. This association is more pronounced for men than it is for women.

Men who report having watched pornography recently–that is, in the past 24 hours–report the highest rates of loneliness. Six in 10 (60 percent) men who watched pornography in the past 24 hours say they have felt lonely or isolated at least once in the past week. In contrast, fewer than four in 10 (38 percent) men who have never watched pornography and 49 percent of men who have watched it but not in the past 24 hours say they have felt lonely in the past week.

Americans who regularly watch pornography also report more frequent feelings of dissatisfaction with their personal appearance. Again, this effect is particularly notable for men. Nearly eight in 10 (78 percent) men who have watched pornography in the past 24 hours say they have felt unhappy about their appearance in the past week. Less than half (44 percent) of men who have never watched pornography and 58 percent of those who have not watched it recently say they have felt unhappy with how they look in the past week.

Men who watch pornography regularly are also more likely to report they frequently feel insecure: 74 percent of men who report having watched pornography in the past 24 hours say they have felt self-conscious or insecure in the past week. Only 45 percent of men who say they have never watched pornography say the same.

Men in their 30s and 40s are the most likely to watch pornography

Percentage of men who say they last watched pornography...

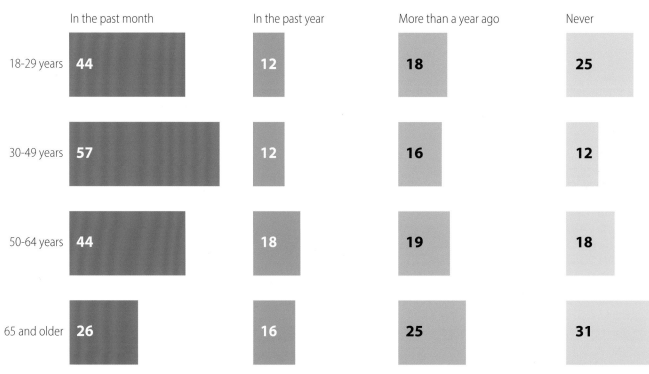

	In the past month	In the past year	More than a year ago	Never
18-29 years	44	12	18	25
30-49 years	57	12	16	12
50-64 years	44	18	19	18
65 and older	26	16	25	31

Men who watch pornography more often feel lonlier, more insecure, and dissatisfied with their personal appearance

Percentage of men who say they felt ... in the past week, by how frequently they watch pornography.

Never watched pornography

Watched, not in the past 24 hours

Watched in the past 24 hours

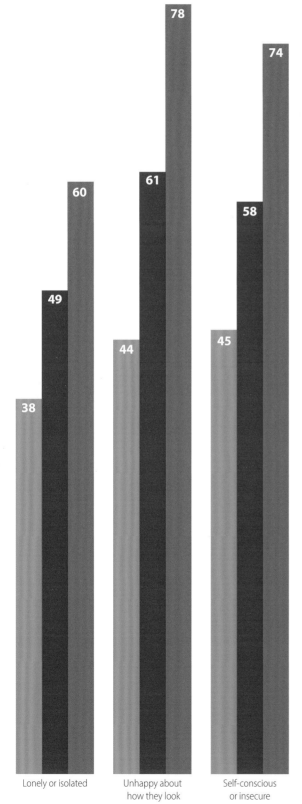

	Lonely or isolated	Unhappy about how they look	Self-conscious or insecure
Never watched	38	44	45
Watched, not in past 24 hours	49	61	58
Watched in past 24 hours	60	78	74

Note: Survey of US Adults [N = 2,007]
Source: American Perspectives Survey, March 2022

Pornography may also contribute to men feeling less satisfied with their sex lives. Only about a quarter (26 percent) of men who report having watched pornography in the past day say they are completely or very satisfied with their sex lives, compared to 41 percent of those who say they have never watched pornography.

The findings here are not conclusive evidence that pornography is causing these problems. Rather, these results show a strong relationship between pornography use and a variety of negative social conditions and circumstances. But it's quite plausible that Americans who are lonelier or feel less confident in their appearance more readily turn to pornography than do those with stronger social ties and greater self-confidence. Results could also be due to confounding variables–such as age, gender, or social class–that are associated with both pornography use and these particular outcomes.

To account for these potentially confounding variables, we ran four separate logistic regression models predicting the following: feelings of loneliness, feelings of personal insecurity, satisfaction with one's appearance, and satisfaction with one's sex life. We find that pornography use remains a significant predictor in each of the four models, even when controlling for important personal characteristics such as age, race and ethnicity, gender, marital status, income, and education.

May 2022

How often do Britons watch porn?

Young people and men watch porn more frequently than women and older Britons, with young men particularly likely to be regular consumers.

Perhaps unsurprisingly, there are considerable age and gender differences in the frequency of watching porn, with men and young people far more likely to be regular watchers and to have watched porn at all.

Three-quarters of British men (76%) say they have ever watched porn, compared to around half of women (53%). Around a third of men (36%) say they watch pornography at least once a week, including 13% who watch porn every day or most days, while just 4% of women say they watch porn at least once a week.

In fact, only 15% of women watch porn with any degree of frequency. Four in ten (38%) say they have seen it before but do not watch it, while another 40% say they have never watched porn at all.

And while younger Britons in general are more likely than older Britons to say they watch porn (48% of under-30s

How frequently do Britons watch pornography?

How frequently, if at all, do you watch pornography? %

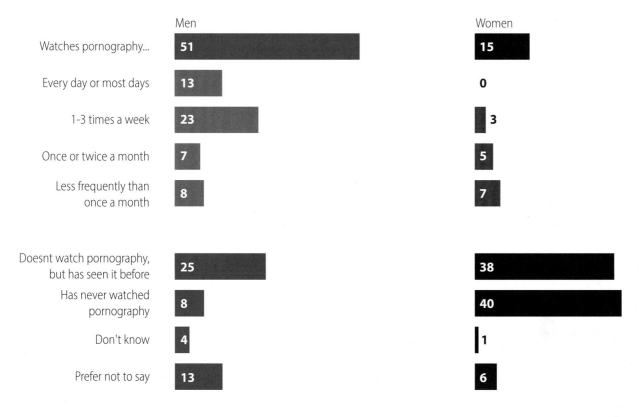

	Men	Women
Watches pornography...	51	15
Every day or most days	13	0
1-3 times a week	23	3
Once or twice a month	7	5
Less frequently than once a month	8	7
Doesnt watch pornography, but has seen it before	25	38
Has never watched pornography	8	40
Don't know	4	1
Prefer not to say	13	6

Source: YouGov

Young women are more likely to watch porn than older women, but to nowhere near the same extent as men

How frequently, if at all, do you watch pornography? % saying they watch pornography

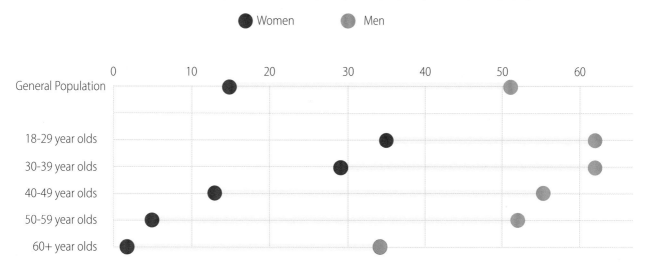

● Women   ● Men

Source: YouGov

compared to 17% of those in their 60s and older), young women are still far less likely to watch porn than young men (35% vs 62%).

Only 35% of women under 30 say they watch porn, compared to just 2% of women aged 60 and older. The young-old divide is far less drastic among men – while 62% of men under 30 say they watch porn, this remains as high as 52% among men in their 50s. Even for men in their 60s and older, a third (34%) say they watch pornography.

Likewise, men are more likely to be frequent watchers of porn. A quarter of men under 30 (25%) watch porn every day or most days, with 13-14% of men in their 30s, 40s and 50s saying the same. A vanishingly small percentage of women of all age groups (2% or fewer) watch porn with this degree of frequency.

1 July 2022

One in three young adults believe porn has affected sexual preferences, survey finds

A third of those surveyed said they were 'surprised' by real sex.

By Steve Richmond

One in three young adults believe watching porn has affected what they find sexually desirable in a partner, according to a study.

The same proportion of 18-24-year-olds polled admitted to being 'surprised' by what sex was like in real life, having watched porn before becoming sexually active.

A quarter of the 1,000 young people asked said having sex was not as good as they expected.

Of those surveyed, 45 per cent feel they would be judged if they did not know how to take part in a sexual act - or if they did not know what one was.

Four in 10 said they felt more pressure to have sex on Valentine's Day.

A spokesperson for the condom company Durex, which commissioned OnePoll to carry out the survey, said: 'The research reveals that among young people there is still a question mark around what sex is or what it should be.

'It poses the question of whether traditional norms, should no longer be the norm.

'Adults should feel more sexually liberated and shouldn't feel pressure to look a particular way or do certain things.

'We want to challenge the conventions that society, ourselves and others place on us - to normalise what real, good sex is and can be for everyone.'

The poll found more than half of young people felt sex education in schools was 'outdated', with one in three saying it was not helpful in navigating modern sexuality.

Six in 10 said they always used protection when having sex, either through condoms, contraceptive pills, IUDs or similar.

However, the same amount also admitted they worry more about running out of money than they do about catching an STI.

More positively, 85 per cent of young adults in the UK said they felt comfortable talking openly about sex with their partner.

But only 33 per cent of those polled were happy to talk with their current partner about how many people they had previously had sex with.

A tenth said they would not disclose their sexual history because they felt the number was too high.

A Durex spokesperson added: 'We hope that conversations about sex, STIs, orientation and consent will become more open and acceptable but understand that some young people might still find these types of conversations anxiety inducing and difficult.

'We think there's a lot of work to do in terms of challenging conventions and enabling conversations about taboos and misconceptions to ensure that everyone feels comfortable talking openly about sex with a partner.'

13 February 2020

Write

Write a paragraph of the meaning of consent.

The real reason that pornography can lead to male sexual dissatisfaction

By Ross Pomeroy

Online pornography has long been lambasted for eroding heterosexual men's sexual and relationship satisfaction, though the truth of this claim is hotly debated amongst social scientists. Evidence exists both for and against it. This suggests that a more nuanced explanation may be needed.

A trio of psychologists – Hio Tong Kuan and Professor Charlene Senn from the University of Windsor, and Assistant Professor Donna M Garcia from California State University - San Bernardino – think they may have one. In a recent article published to the journal *SAGE Open*, they propose that the unrealistic depictions of sex, female partners, and relationships commonly seen in pornography can warp men's expectations of real-life sex. When heterosexual men expect sex with their partners to be just like the staged fantasies they see on the Internet, this can lead to dissatisfaction and even lower their well-being.

To test this hypothesis, the researchers anonymously surveyed 195 heterosexual men aged 18 to 58 using Amazon's Mechanical Turk, asking them about their pornography habits, the ideal sex they would like to have in their relationships, and the characteristics of the sex they are actually having in their relationships. The researchers also gauged their sexual satisfaction, life satisfaction, and general self-esteem.

Reviewing the results, the authors found that when heterosexual men desired sex to be just like they viewed in stereotypical pornography – degrading to women, with attractive, groomed partners, performing vigorous intercourse – and the actual sex they were having failed to reach those impractical ideals, they were less sexually satisfied and expressed lower self-esteem.

'The exaggerated and unrealistic sexual practices featured in contemporary [pornography] likely sets up an impossible or undesirable expectation of female partners, which in turn produces discrepant sexual experiences for heterosexual men and dissatisfaction with their experiences and their partners,' the researchers summarized.

So, according to the study, pornography-viewing alone doesn't lead to sexual dissatisfaction. It's only when men expect real-life sex to be like porn that problems arise.

There are a couple primary ways to counter this. For one, comprehensive sex education for teenagers and young-adults should instruct students about the unrealistic, performative nature of pornography so they can understand what they are viewing when they almost inevitably watch it. That way that can approach their own sexual exploits with proper expectations. Second, consumers of pornography can seek out, and the industry can produce, more realistic pornography which depicts consent, actors with more 'average' bodies, and respect for female partners.

12 March 2022

How watching porn can hurt your mental health and self-esteem

Research indicates that consuming porn is linked with more negative body image, lower self-esteem, and poorer mental health.

Did you know that porn can hurt your mental health, including distorting people's perceptions of sex, intimacy, body image, and sexual performance?

Research indicates that consuming porn is linked with more negative body image, lower self-esteem, and poorer mental health.

And not only that, research is shedding light on a previously little-known fact about porn: it's harmful to consumers' brains. Thanks to all the research that has been done in recent years, people are finally starting to realize how toxic pornography can be.

The research on how porn affects how consumers view themselves, their partner, and their relationships, in general, is becoming prevalent. When people consume porn, it not only warps their view of others, but it can also twist their view of themselves. Here's how.

Insecurity and mental health impacts

Studies have found that when people engage in an ongoing pattern of 'self-concealment,' which is when they do things they're not proud of and keep them a secret, it can not only hurt their relationships and leave them feeling lonely but can also make them more vulnerable to mental health issues.

In fact, a number of peer-reviewed studies have found a link between pornography consumption and mental health outcomes like depression, anxiety, loneliness, lower life satisfaction, and poorer self-esteem and overall mental health.

These studies have found that these links are particularly strong when pornography is consumed to try to escape negative emotions and also when pornography consumption becomes heavy and compulsive. According to another study performed in the United States, researchers found a significant bi-directional association between pornography and loneliness, prompting them to conclude:

'Results revealed that the association between loneliness and viewing pornography was positive and significant…those who viewed pornography were more likely to experience loneliness, and those who were experiencing loneliness were more likely to view pornography. These findings are consistent with research linking pornography use to negative affect.'

Although it's fairly common for consumers to use porn as an escape mechanism or self-soothing technique, research indicates that those who consumed pornography to avoid uncomfortable emotions had some of the lowest reports of emotional and mental wellbeing. Another study examined the relationship between the frequency of online pornography consumption and mental health problems, particularly in the context of 'experiential avoidance' or trying to avoid negative emotions. The study found that frequent pornography consumption was significantly related to greater depression, anxiety, and stress as well as poorer social functioning.

And in yet another study, researchers at Columbia University, Yale University, and UCLA, found a link between compulsive pornography consumption and poorer mental health, low self-esteem, and poor attachment in relationships. The authors concluded:

'In this paper, we propose that pornography use has the potential to become addictive and might be conceptualized as a behavioural addiction… individuals who scored higher on the Problematic Pornography Use Scale reported poorer mental health and self-esteem, and more insecure close relationships than those who scored lower, illustrating the negative emotional correlates of problematic pornography use.'

Sex can be great; comparing it to porn isn't

But your relationship with yourself isn't the only thing harmed by porn. Your relationship with others can be, too.

To start, dozens of studies have repeatedly shown that porn consumers tend to have lower relationship satisfaction and lower relationship quality.

Porn consumers tend to experience more negative communication with their partners, feel less dedicated to their relationships, have a more difficult time making adjustments in their relationships, are less sexually satisfied, and commit more infidelity. Research also shows that porn consumers tend to become less committed to their partners, less satisfied in their relationships, and more accepting of cheating.

Meanwhile, partners of porn consumers also report negative effects, such as lower self-esteem, worse relationship quality, and less sexual satisfaction. Research also suggests that porn consumption can undermine trust in a relationship and fuel couple conflict.

Obviously, relationship problems like these are not new and are not solely caused by porn. Yet, research shows that porn can play a substantial role in fuelling these issues – and that's not something that should be ignored.

Choose love, not porn.

If you have been struggling to quit an unwanted porn habit, please know that you're not alone. It can feel really lonely and frustrating, but there is hope. While research shows that consuming porn can fuel the cycle of loneliness, research also shows that it is possible to overcome a porn habit and its negative effects. According to one study of individuals trying to quit porn, researchers found that shame actually predicted increased pornography consumption while guilt predicted sustainable change.

So if you're trying to give up porn to improve your mental health and self-esteem, be kind to yourself and be patient with your progress. Like anything, it takes time for the brain to recover, but daily efforts make a big difference in the long run.

The above information is reprinted with kind permission from Fight the New Drug.

Fight the New Drug is a non-religious and non-legislative organisation that exists to provide individuals the opportunity to make an informed decision regarding pornography by raising awareness on its harmful effects using only science, facts, and personal accounts.

Research citations and more information can be found at www.fightthenewdrug.org

© Fight the New Drug, Inc 2023

www.fightthenewdrug.org

When does watching porn become a problem?

By Ian Richards

- Porn is now a much more mainstream component of many people's healthy sex lives, however for some it presents a problem

- Therapist Ian Richards, specialist in porn and sex addiction, explores the signs and effects of problematic porn use

Twenty years ago, saying the word porn in public may well have resulted in raised eyebrows and silent murmurings. The once British stiff upper lip attitude towards sex has now evolved and our cultural attitude towards it has changed. Pornography is now a more mainstream pastime, with users across the planet finding it an easy and, in particular, a private way to satisfy their sexual needs. However, there is a darker and more sinister side of pornography. It can and often does have a devastating effect on the viewer's mental health.

Before I explain why, it's probably worth taking a look at some recent statistics which will give you an idea of how big this problem currently is.

- On average, there are 68 million search queries relating to pornography every day

- Shockingly, over 115,000 are related to child pornography

- Internet pornography statistics show there are roughly 4.2 million pornographic websites that make up 12% of the total internet content

- Pornographic pages have 372 million hits daily

- Cybersex/pornography addiction is a common cause of separation and divorce

- It is believed that it hinders the development of healthy sexuality amongst adolescents

- It is believed to affect between 5 and 8% of the population

The Times suggested in a recent survey that 58% of the British population watch porn. Here are the results of the survey compiled in 2019.

- 12% of all websites on the internet are pornographic

- 1 in 3 porn viewers are women

- Internet porn revenues worldwide are a staggering £4.2 billion per annum and are estimated to be a £13 billion industry

- 25% of search engine requests are porn-related

- The average age that a child first sees porn is 11

- 20,000 participants were surveyed in Australia and 4.4% of men felt they had an addiction to porn with woman at 1.2%

When does watching porn become a problem?

So why is it that such a simple bit of fun, within the privacy of someone's four walls, could become an addiction?

For some watching porn is harmless fun and enjoyable, but for others it might be used compulsively. Compulsive or problematic porn use can act as a self-soother for someone who is suffering with anxiety or depression. It is also associated with someone who has deep-rooted underlying issues that haven't yet been resolved.

While it's not believed that watching porn can cause depression, in my experience many clients who come to see me with a porn addiction issue often do present with anxiety, depression or both. The problem here of course is that it's counterproductive. You watch porn to self-soothe then afterwards have feelings of guilt and shame which inevitably leads you back to watching porn again – this is called the addictive cycle. Continually viewing porn can cause sexually compulsive and dependent behaviours. It can also result in the development of sex addiction.

The neuroscience of addictive behaviours

Dopamine is a neurotransmitter (chemical messenger) used by our nervous system which sends signals between our nerve cells. It is produced in the dopaminergic neurons in the ventral tegmental area (VTA) of the midbrain. It plays a number of roles in the body such as body movement, mood and behaviours, amongst others. If there is a deficiency with dopamine it can cause a variety of issues; Parkinson's disease and addiction are just two of many.

Dopamine is also the control centre of the reward system of the brain. When it's released it mediates our pleasure experiences and we enjoy things such as eating chocolate or having sex. Exercising also releases dopamine and the more you release this chemical the more you crave it. So, the pleasure and reward will create the motivation to repeat the behaviour. You come home from work at night and have a glass of wine with your meal, then it's a glass of wine while you're cooking the meal, then its whole bottle and so on.

Dopamine informs the brain that it has enjoyed the experience and craves more of the same and this is where the addiction cycle begins. Porn addiction rewires the brain, and the more you watch it the more the dopamine gets stronger and stronger. Over time this will cause you to find the videos less arousing, leading you to become desensitised. I have had clients who have spent all night and day watching porn without reaching climax. Many develop erectile dysfunction (ED) as they lose any sense of arousal.

If someone is addicted to porn, they may lose interest in other healthier activities that they once enjoyed. They will start to neglect things that were once important to them like family and friends. Work can become secondary as they will often feel mentally consumed every day. This can then lead to relationship issues, infidelity, separation, and divorce.

I have had clients who have suffered loss of employment leading to financial difficulties. Porn addiction can have a devastating effect. They will have probably tried to cease their behaviour on numerous occasions, only to find themselves falling back into their addiction.

There is also a growing concern about the rise of porn use in adolescents and, yes, teenage girls are watching porn too. It can hinder the development of a healthy sexuality and can create distorted attitudes around sex. Just as when someone takes drugs, the more an individual participates the stronger the urges will develop.

What are the side effects and warning signs of porn addiction?

- Lowered desire to have sexual interactions with a partner
- Noticing it becoming more difficult to maintain an erection and eventually potentially suffering from (ED) erectile dysfunction
- Noticing that porn and masturbation is the only way you can manage to orgasm
- Noticing the occurrence of relationship difficulties
- Using alcohol or drugs to booster sexual arousal
- Being drawn to viewing various paraphilias
- Visiting illegal sites
- Feelings of shame
- Feelings of low self-worth
- Experiencing lack of motivation and increasing levels of procrastination
- Decreased memory and the ability to focus

Can the porn addiction cycle be reversed?

Quite simply, yes. Having long periods of abstinence together with therapy does help the brain's physiology return to a normal state.

Developing one's self-awareness and learning how manage negative feelings in a healthier way can help on this difficult journey. While this may take some time there is increasing evidence that many individuals suffering from this issue can return to a normal healthy relationship with sex.

10 February 2021

Is pornography to blame for rise in 'rape culture'?

Analysis: experts split on whether easy access to porn has fuelled sexual harassment, abuse and assault among young people.

By Nicola Davis, Science correspondent

The harrowing reports of sexism and assaults in schools detailed on the everyonesinvited.uk website has fuelled concerns of a 'rape culture' in educational settings.

The disclosures have raised concerns that easy access to pornography is part of the problem.

It's a complex issue – and the answer is far from clear cut. Some experts urge caution about making links, while others say porn is undermining the notion of consent.

While access to online porn is rising, experts say it is not clear whether sexual harassment, abuse and assault among young people is similarly increasing – as may be expected from a simple link between the two.

Roger Ingham, a professor of health and community psychology and director of the Centre for Sexual Health Research at the University of Southampton, said greater publicity, increased awareness of what was acceptable, and even a feeling that victims would be taken more seriously, could fuel more reporting of rape or other sexual offences.

Furthermore, even if perpetrators were found to watch porn, it would remain unclear whether porn was to blame, Ingham said. 'It could be, for example, that those who are more inclined to commit "offences" are also more likely to access porn, so a correlation between the two cannot be assumed to indicate direct cause.'

Another problem is that even if porn is having a negative influence, controlling who sees what is difficult, both for governments and parents, while a 'rape culture' is likely to fuelled by many factors.

'There will always be a small proportion of young people with serious issues in maintain[ing] responsible and respectful social interactions and relationships,' Ingham said. 'It would be very naive to attribute negative behaviours to just one factor, such as porn access.'

Mark McCormack, a professor of sociology at the University of Roehampton, agreed there was a lack of evidence that sexual harassment in schools was less common in the past, adding that new technology often caused concerns – such as the worries in previous decades about whether violent films could lead to increased violence among young viewers.

According to McCormack, a key aspect of porn that needs to be explored is why people watch it, noting that while it might be linked to negative outcomes in some, for others it could be an important way to explore their sexual identity.

In addition, he said research had found those who watch porn were not more sexist than those who did not. Where porn did cause problems, he said, it tended to be indirect, for example tensions with a partner owing to non-disclosure of porn-watching – it was not necessarily the case that those who watch porn then wished to act out what they saw.

'My concern when we go to porn as the problem, that just focuses on, in a sense, a technology and a thing, and not actually the much deeper and broader issues we need to address: sexual harassment, sexism, gender inequality,' he said.

But others say pornography is problematic.

'Unfortunately the pornography that is widely available online can be graphic and aggressive, and the women depicted on some of the sites are getting younger and younger, borderline to being illegal,' said Dr Elena Martellozzo, an associate professor in criminology at Middlesex University.

Martellozzo added that the message that men had a 'right' to women's bodies undermined the notion of consent. 'This is the definition of rape culture in a nutshell,' she said.

According to research by Martellozzo and colleagues based on data collected in between 2015 and 2016 and published this year, 65% of 15- to 16-year-olds in the UK reported seeing pornography, with porn more commonly seen by boys.

Just over half of the 241 of boys in the study aged 11-16 who had seen porn said they thought it was 'realistic' compared with 39% of 195 girls in the study who had seen porn, with 44% of boys and 29% of girls saying it had given them ideas to try out.

Martellozzo added the concerns were not a 'moral panic', and that she and others are working towards controlling what was available online.

'We can't of course generalise and say that everybody that watches porn would move on into wanting to act out what they had seen, but we do know that some young men do want to act out what they have seen and therefore expecting girls to respond to their request, respond to their desire of performance,' she said.

Dr Leila Frodsham, a consultant gynaecologist and spokesperson for the Royal College of Obstetricians and Gynaecologists, said there could be other consequences of young people watching porn. 'One knock-on effect that people might not consider is girls and women feeling their genitalia should look a certain way because that's what they have seen in the mass media or that's what boys are seeing through pornography and telling girls,' she said.

'We are very concerned by reports that labiaplasty rates – surgery to change the look of the vagina – are increasing in under 18s, especially as there is no scientific reason to support its practice.'

Experts agree better sex education is crucial. 'What is needed is open, serious, honest conversations about sexual consent, about sex in relationships and about the broader context and the complexities [of sex],' McCormack said.

Martellozzo added there needed to be a shift in emphasis away from blaming victims of sexual harassment and abuse and instead a focus on perpetrators. 'The emphasis here is really to educate the individual, and demonstrate to them that the effects of their choice of language or action is huge,' she said.

Frodsham also stressed the need for better education. 'Pornography provides children and young people with a false impression of what to expect when they do start having sex, and can set unrealistic goals for boys and girls when it comes to exploring their sexuality,' she said.

'It's widely disputed whether porn directly influences a rape culture. What is clear is that the matter of consent and what a healthy relationship looks like needs to be tackled head on in the school curriculum, so that boys and girls learn to respect one another and girls know to raise the alarm if they do experience abuse.'

29 March 2021

Write

Write a paragraph or two about what a healthy relationship looks like to you. How is consent a vital part of a healthy relationship?

How the pandemic has made young people more vulnerable to risky online sexual trade

By Elena Martellozzo & Paula Bradbury

The existence of OnlyFans – a subscription-based social media platform where users can sell and/or purchase original content from softcore or X rated – predates the COVID-19 pandemic lockdown of 2020, but its popularity and notoriety has increased significantly over the last year. OnlyFans came to our attention through celebrity endorsements, other social media platforms and apps, as well as the BBC Three documentary entitled *Nudes4Sale*.

This British investigative documentary revealed how thousands of people across the world – including celebrities, ordinary members of the public including, more concerningly, teenagers – are making a healthy profit from selling self-generated sexual content for cash through the interactive platform OnlyFans. On OnlyFans you earn money by gaining member subscriptions and by generating content that people want to pay for. Lauren, one of the girls featured in the documentary, told the Times Radio in a recent interview that she earned £15,000 in her first month of being on the site.

However, these kinds of success stories are unique and only experienced by a few, leaving a significant number vulnerable to a darker side of OnlyFans, and the manipulative and predatory behaviours of individuals that operate within it. Vulnerable young people may find themselves using sites like this one to support their living, particularly during the lockdown period, which has completely eclipsed parts of the hospitality industry and other opportunities to finds work. Sasha, who struggled financially and has a history of mental health issues, told BBC4 that she earned few hundred pounds a month on OnlyFans, using sex toys and collaborating with other performers.

With a fast-growing subscriber-base of more than 200,000 new members every 24 hours, it's easy to see how enthusiastic endorsements by the likes of Beyoncé and Cardi B make OnlyFans an attractive site for young people.

What the endorsements don't show, though, is that OnlyFans is a fiercely competitive market where young people, often women, can fall into a risky cycle. In an interview with Channel 4, Dr Elena Martellozzo said that young women are compelled to raise their game by sharing more and more of their bodies, and perform sexual acts requested by subscribers to maintain their interest, increase their popularity and earn more money.

The women in the *Nudes4Sale* documentary had all received messages from subscribers asking them to participate in offline sex acts. One of the girls interviewed in the documentary, Lauren, admitted that she received messages offering £5,000 for sex. While Lauren can afford to say no, many less successful young women – potentially young teenage girls – might not be able to, and might be at risk of being lured into danger with the promise of money.

And during a pandemic, having an income is more crucial than ever. Whilst the site might have changed sex work forever by creating a safe environment for sex workers to engage with their clients, it has opened up a new arena for inexperienced young people who are lured into making quick cash for kink.

'It's impossible to say precisely how lockdown is impacting our behaviour and what the side effects will be', wrote Anne Marie Tomchak in a recent piece in Glamour, 'but there are already indications that more nudes are being requested and sent during this time as people increase their digital interactions while staying at home, and OnlyFans reports a spike in activity.'

OnlyFans sparked a global media response to rising concerns of adolescent online risk-taking, and the legal ramifications of creating, distributing and possessing sexual images of a minor – laws, which children themselves are no less impervious to.

A 2020 report published by the Internet Watch Foundation revealed that they have identified a 44% increase (of all intercepted content) in the number of self-generated indecent images produced by children, of which the most prolific age group is girls between 11 and 13.

COVID-19 and child protection

The COVID-19 global pandemic has not only revealed our vulnerabilities to biological viral threats, but also to our inability to protect our children online.

In the midst of a lockdown, COVID-19 has facilitated a greater opportunity for digital immersion. While the internet opens up a plethora of positive opportunities for individual growth and self-acceptance, there is also the potential for great harm to be caused against the most vulnerable in our communities – children and young people.

Immature cognitive development and reduced capacity to self-regulate leaves children at risk from criminal accountability, sexual predators, and the dark side of the online sex industry. With the easy opportunity to view pornography and violent content at the click of a button, there's also the easy opportunity to produce it, and sell it to those with a sexual predilection in children.

In 2021, the online marketplace for sharing sexual images for cash is no longer dominated by the sex industry and adult sex workers. It is a phenomenon that goes beyond regulation and is being utilised also by teenagers as purveyors for their self-production of nude, semi-nude, on-demand kink images and videos for online clients.

Andy Burrows, head of child safety online policy at the NSPCC, said: 'We are concerned that there are risks to be

associated with user-generated explicit abuse content sites, such as OnlyFans, which are worthy of substantive academic focus. This relates to children being readily able to access inappropriate and sexually explicit content, both on the site itself but also as a result of user generated content being posted as "trailers" to social networks.'

What can parents do?

We would encourage all parents to familiarise themselves with social media, particularly those platforms which are popular with young people. Don't assume that your teen will not visit sites such as OnlyFans.

Parents need to be aware that social media apps such as Instagram, Facebook and Snapchat are the most commonly used platforms for sex offenders to target and groom children. The NSPCC found that during the first three months of the UK's 2020 lockdown, Instagram was used 37% of recorded cases of sexual communication with a child.

Tiktok has aggressively responded to the high volume of Onlyfans members who prolifically use their platform to advertise links to their accounts and content by introducing stricter community guidelines, but as we have seen in our research, a large volume falls beneath the radar which includes sexually explicit information about sex acts, fetishes and violence. Many Onlyfans members simply create a new account once removed.

If you discover that your child is actively engaging with such sites, don't make them feel guilty. It's not your child's fault. Children often visit such sites through peer pressure, general curiosity or simply by accident. However, do prevent them from accessing it in future. It may not make you a popular parent, but it's what needs to be done to keep your child safe, both online and offline. We recommend the following:

- If you don't have a filter on your child's laptop or home computer already, make sure you get one as soon as you can

- Browse your teen's tracking history. If you see OnlyFans on there, that's a red flag

- Scan your credit card for any charges that look like they may be from OnlyFans

- If you suspect your teen has been on the site, have an honest discussion with them about online safety

- Talk to your teen, in general, about the damaging effects of pornography

- Make sure your child understands that they never know who they're talking to online, and that by sharing personal information they're putting themselves at risk.

Stumbling across inappropriate content can have significant adverse impacts for children and young people. This includes distorting their view of sex and relationships, and potentially having a desensitising effect for some young people.

Online pornography is increasingly identified as an influence on children's and young people's sexual lives. Whether we like or not, pornography is recognised as an important part of young people's sexual socialisation and it is crucial to have open discussions with them about this. The existence of sites such as OnlyFans should be included in the discussions.

2 March 2021

Activity

This article includes tips for parents to protect their children against viewing inappropriate content and grooming. What tips would you give to a young person to stay safe online? How can someone find help if they have viewed something that they are not comfortable with?

The above information is reprinted with kind permission from the London School of Economics and Political Science.
© LSE 2023

www.lse.ac.uk

Big porn, human trafficking, and the global sex-trade; it isn't a few bad apples, the whole tree is rotten

Interview with Rose Kalemba, words by Tom Farr

On the 10th February, the BBC published the story of Rose Kalemba, a young woman from Ohio who had been through what anybody would describe as a truly horrific series of events. For anyone unfamiliar with the story, as a 14-year-old girl Rose was kidnapped at knife-point, stabbed, and then raped over a period of 12 hours while one of the men filmed the attack. In the following months, she suffered at the hands of disbelieving authorities and an unsympathetic justice system, and things became so bad she attempted to end her own life.

The brutality of this is of course shocking in and of itself, but the tragedy didn't end there for Rose. Several months after the attack, Rose was made aware of a link being passed around by people from her school: a link which she was tagged in by name. Upon opening the link, she was directed to Pornhub. What she saw induced a wave of nausea and panic: videos of her assault and rape had been uploaded, with titles such as *'teen crying and getting slapped around'*, *'teen getting destroyed'*, *'passed out teen'*. One of these videos had been viewed over 400,000 times. Rose pleaded with Pornhub via email to take the videos down, but they ignored her every single time. Until one day, she decided to threaten them with legal action – not knowing whether it would work and not knowing whether it was even something she could follow through with – and the videos quickly disappeared. But the trauma remained.

I first spoke with Rose in the summer of 2019. As she talked me through her story I was struck by how courageous she was, and is, for coming forward in an effort to shine a light on just how rotten the porn industry is. 10 years had passed,

and she had begun her recovery process, but it was the prospect of other girls and women suffering as she had, and Pornhub subsequently profiting, that had motivated her to speak out.

This had come as a response to Pornhub rolling out a 'Save-the-Bees' campaign drawing attention to the environmental issues caused by a dwindling bee population. If this sounds like an absurd campaign for a porn website to be involved in, you're not wrong. But Rose was angered by this; the profiteers of her exploitation seemed to be portraying themselves as a progressive, environmentally conscious and forward-thinking organisation that happened to also host porn videos. She was furious. And so should we all be.

Speaking to me now, Rose tells me:

Pornhub are a human trafficking hub wrapped up in shiny faux-woke gift wrap and topped with a bow- all an illusion to distract us from seeing what they really are.

This is a damning, but wholly accurate, indictment of what type of company Pornhub really is. While some people may object to terms such as 'human trafficking' being used, this is not just emotive language to garner a reaction. Last year the owners of the company GirlsDoPorn were charged with human trafficking offences, and found guilty of lying to and coercing young women to perform on camera for them. There was industry-wide outrage at this supposed 'bad apple', and a move towards distancing themselves from the company. It should come as a surprise therefore, or perhaps not, to find that Pornhub is still hosting these videos and profiting off them.

And this is not confined to GirlsDoPorn either. To understand these links, we need to look at the Trafficking Victims Protection Act 2000 (TVPA), a federal statute passed in the US in 2000. When people think about what trafficking entails, often it is the image of people being forcibly shipped across borders into situations of domestic and/or sexual servitude and slavery. This, sadly, is of course common. But the TVPA goes further in defining the context in which trafficking can take place. Section 102(a) TVPA defines domestic sex trafficking as:

'A commercial sex act is induced by force, fraud, or coercion, or in which the person induced to perform such act has not attained 18 years of age.'

This legislation takes the idea of trafficking beyond that of being a solely international or cross-border issue. It sets out criteria that where a commercial sex act takes place through force or coercion, it constitutes trafficking. Under this definition, huge quantities of porn are implicated.

Exploitation in the porn industry

'I was threatened that if I did not do the scene I was going to get sued for lots of money.'

'[I] told them to stop but they wouldn't stop until I started to cry and ruined the scene.'

'He told me that I had to do it and if I can't, he would charge me and I would lose any other bookings I had because I would make his agency look bad.'

These quotes, from survivors of the porn industry, highlight that force, coercion and abuse are key elements of getting women to 'perform' in the desired ways. Make no mistake, this is sex trafficking. As Rose rightly points out, Pornhub is a hub for this material, and consequently is complicit in the propagation of human trafficking both domestically and across the globe. Not only is the production and consumption of porn on the rise, but so is 'gonzo' porn, featuring frequent violence such as gagging, slapping and choking. In this context it is all but guaranteed that the abuse and coercion in porn If this sounds far fetched, why not hear what the performers themselves have to say about it.

Often there are attempts to separate this explicitly abusive and violent porn from so-called 'ethical' porn, but this is a contradictory notion. Porn is the wholesale commodification of human sexuality, sold for profit, which disproportionately negatively affects the women involved in the industry. It matters not that 'some' porn is allegedly ethical, because it is still part of the wider industry that functions by commodifying abuse into a consumable product. This is something that Rose herself discussed with me:

I don't believe the porn industry could ever be ethical, because the potential for abuse is far too great. Neither sex nor porn are human rights that anyone is entitled to. The safety and lives of the victims involved, largely women and girls, however, IS a human right that must be protected at all costs.

Further to that, Rose was also keen to stress that the exploitation extends beyond Pornhub, and into the industry at large:

A lot of people try to argue that while big companies like Pornhub are exploitative, independently produced porn is not. But when my story first went public, I received dozens of messages from young women who were forced by their traffickers or in some cases abusive boyfriends or husbands to produce content for websites like Onlyfans, Manyvids, and others. One nineteen year old woman told me that her abuser forced her to keep a smile on her face while he violated her and made her do things to herself on camera against her will. **The truth is that the problem with the industry isn't 'a few bad apples'- it's a rotten tree.**

When our eyes are opened to the exploitation and violence that occurs at every level of the porn industry, it becomes obvious that thrives on a destructive power imbalance: men wielding abusive power over women, which is often repackaged as being empowering or 'sex positive'.

Moving beyond porn specifically for a moment, the effect this has had on the lives of women within other aspects of the commercial sex-trade, specifically the system of prostitution, is disastrous. Pornography has normalised violence and coercion, and has many links to prostitution. It doesn't require great feats of imagination to realise that as porn continues to propagate harmful attitudes towards sex, men will want to act these out on women within prostitution, and indeed, the research confirms this. The links are all too clear to Rose as well:

As women, we must remember not to fall for the lie that our own objectification is empowering. Something is only empowering if it gains us real, tangible power. If sexualizing violence was truly 'empowering' then men would have been lining up to be the target of it decades ago.

Once again, Rose cuts through all the noise with an acute awareness of just how oppressive and exploitative the porn industry is. It has convinced women that their own empowerment lies in sexual objectification through porn or prostitution.

In that vein, I will draw this post to a close with some final words from Rose. It is a privilege to know her, and CEASE UK stands alongside her and all other victims and survivors of sexual exploitation and male violence against women, and we are fundamentally committed to seeing an end to the abhorrent profiteering off human misery and despair propagated by the porn industry.

What people who watch porn don't understand is, they might think that they aren't harming anyone, but this is plain wrong. They are the ones enabling and creating a demand for the exploitation. This absolutely makes them complicit.

24 February 2020

The above information is reprinted with kind permission from CEASE.
© 2023 CEASE / Centre to End All Sexual Exploitation

www.cease.org.uk

What is revenge porn? 5 Things you should know from the experts

What is Revenge porn? Sounds scary doesn't it? Here, Carmel Glassbrook from the Revenge Porn Helpline breaks down the top 5 things you need to know about revenge porn from her experience working with the organisation:

1. It's not always about 'revenge' and it's not really porn.

So, the story goes; 'Boy meets girl. Girl sends boy nudes. Girl and boy break up, then, in fit of rage and jealousy, boy shares nudes all over the internet.'

…Well, not always. Catfishing and sextortion are also a reality. This refers to the horrible situation some people find themselves in when they think they're having sexual exchanges over webcam with an unbelievably sexy person. Only to later get blackmailed with the video of them masturbating for £££!

At the Revenge Porn helpline, we've even had cases where nudes were shared in adoration. The perpetrators are often completely flabbergasted that anyone would consider what they are doing was wrong: 'But I think she's really hot and I just wanted more pics of her!'

The word 'porn' is also a misnomer. Porn is something sexy and enjoyable. FYI, having your intimate images spitefully shared is not sexy. Nor is sharing someone else's nudes… for any reason!

2. The difference between 'sexting' and 'revenge porn'?

Revenge porn is the non-consensual sharing of intimate images of anyone OVER the age of 18.

Sexting usually refers to intimate image sharing of anyone UNDER the age of 18.

If you are under 18 and share nudes of anyone over 18, you could be criminalised under the revenge porn law. But (stay with me, it's about to get even more confusing) due to a law created in 1978, a naked image of anyone under the age of 18 is an indecent image of a child, which could carry quite a substantial punishment for possession or production.

SO, you can have sex at age 16 but if you take a nude you are committing a very serious crime. Clear as mud, right?!

The Revenge Porn Helpline supports people over the age of 18 only. Not least because we have to search for, view and report images and we couldn't do that if the image is of someone under 18, because that would be illegal. Thankfully, the IWF (partner in UK SIC) are very successful in removing indecent images of under 18s from the internet.

3. What does the revenge porn law cover?

When it was passed in April 2015, the law made the non-consensual sharing of intimate images a crime, carrying a potential custodial sentence of up to 2 years. The prosecution has to prove an 'intent to cause distress' - as if having your nudes all over Facebook isn't proof enough.

Recently the law has been updated to include 'threatening' to share people's nudes. A massive win for us on the Helpline! Too often, callers have been turned away from the police because the person hasn't shared anything, yet! Threats and blackmail were already covered by the 'Malicious Communications Act', however this generally had

a poor response. To make it easier and clearer for police to prosecute – this has now been included. But there is always room for improvement.

Unfortunately the laws are most effective if the victim and perpetrator are in the same country. In theory, someone in America committing RP against someone British should be simple. Most US states have a similar law so why wouldn't they be arrested there!? However, there are a lot of factors that get in the way – lack of police resources being one. Despite this, it is possible to prosecute a perpetrator of RP across the pond. Unfortunately, if the perpetrator was elsewhere – in the Philippines for example, it's a completely different story.

4. Where is revenge porn?

You'd think that seeing as it's illegal to upload this content, it shouldn't be anywhere online. WRONG! The images themselves are not illegal and sites are not breaking the law by hosting them. There are still dedicated RP websites moving their hosting sites so often that they're impossible to catch.

The dark web hosts some disturbing content, where RP might feel like the least of our worries. RP is shared on social media daily but there have been some incredible moves to tackle this. Facebook and Instagram have implemented a hashing technology. Meaning if an image is removed for being RP, they will code this image so it can't be shared on their platforms again! Fear not, there have been a few notable prosecutions globally for running abhorrent RP sites – so it has been done before!

5. What should I do?

The best thing anyone can do is not add to this culture of humiliation. If someone has trusted you with their nudes, don't share them. If you split up with someone, delete their pics. It's really simple when you put it like that.

If your images have been shared – don't panic! Get some support from a loved one and report it to the police. No social media accept RP on their platforms, so take control and report the content.

Most importantly, call the Helpline. We will provide a helping hand to support you through this, giving you emotional and practical advice. Lastly, don't be a bystander – if you see or know someone is being abused in this way – help them by always reporting it!

May 2021

Revenge Porn Helpline

Helpline: 0345 6000 459

Email: help@revengepornhelpline.org.uk

Website: www.revengepornhelpline.org.uk

Can the law stop internet bots from undressing you?

An article from The Conversation.

By Jo-Ann Pattinson, Postdoctoral Research Fellow, University of Leeds & Subhajit Basu, Associate Professor in Cyberlaw; Chair, BILETA, University of Leeds

Imagine that you upload a photograph of yourself on holiday to your favourite social media platform. You are dressed in a swimsuit and you are smiling at the camera. Now imagine later coming across this image while scrolling through your newsfeed. You recognise your face and the background and it looks like your photo, but in this image, you are completely naked. There are some inconsistencies – you do not recognise the body in the image – but it is convincing nonetheless.

This might sound like a scene from a *Black Mirror* episode but is in fact a real possibility thanks to tools available on the social media app Telegram, which allows users to upload innocent images of a (clothed) person, and request that the person in the image is 'digitally undressed' for a fee. Telegram has more than 400 million active monthly users.

While Telegram operates predominantly as a messaging app, it facilitates autonomous programmes (referred to as 'bots'), one of which is able to digitally synthesise these deepfake naked images.

Deepfake detection company Sensity recently published research into Telegram. They found that 70% of Telegram users use its deepfake bot to target women and that, as of the end of July 2020, at least 104,852 fake nude images had been shared in an 'image collections' channel available on the app. The number of user-requested images which have been publicly shared is likely to be much higher. The ease

with which such 'image manipulation' may be carried out without the knowledge of its victims is alarming.

So: is the use of deepfake bots to produce pseudo naked images legal?

Underage pictures

The Telegram bot has been linked to reports of images which appear to be of underage girls. In this case – if the person in the image is underage – the legal position is clear. Images of real children which are altered to appear nude or sexually explicit are internationally unlawful. The Convention on the Rights of the Child, ratified by 196 countries, requires parties to the convention to take steps to protect children from being sexually exploited and being used in the production of pornographic material.

As long as Telegram removes reported indecent images of children, Telegram is not culpable under current international legal frameworks if a user uses the deepfake bot to produce an indecent image of a child. But it is doubtful that this law makes the bot itself unlawful.

In the UK, international obligations to protect children from sexual exploitation are bolstered by laws prohibiting the production of sexual pseudo-imagery, such as a photoshopped image of a young person appearing naked. The Protection of Children Act (1978) prohibits the creation and distribution of such an image, and Section 160 of the Criminal Justice Act (1988) also makes it an offence for a person to have a pseudo-image portraying an indecent image of a child in their possession.

What about adults?

For women and men over the age of 18, the production of a sexual pseudo-image of a person is not in itself illegal under international law or in the UK, even if it is produced and distributed without the consent of the person portrayed in the image.

This is, as usual, a case of the law playing catch-up. International laws created to protect privacy do not necessarily protect people from this type of abuse. Article 8 of the European Convention on Human Rights, which provides a right to respect for a person's 'private and family life, home and correspondence', has been used as the basis for domestic laws throughout the UK and Europe to protect photographs, but only if the original image remains unaltered.

The Telegram bot therefore exploits a legal gap when it comes to deepfake imagery of adults (Telegram did not respond to our questions about the bot and the images it produces, nor to Sensity's enquiries as of the publication of the report). While there are laws that can protect adults from sexual exploitation and abuse via social media, these laws are not as robust as those which protect children. They do not apply to images produced by Telegram AI-bots.

For example, in the UK, the phenomenon of revenge porn – non-consensual sharing of naked and sexual images – is prohibited under the Criminal Courts and Justice Act (2015). But this does not cover situations where an original or standard image is altered to appear sexual or naked. The distribution of a Telegram-type image would not be captured under the revenge pornography provisions, even

if the person creating the image meant to cause harm and distress to the victim. Under these provisions an essential component is that the perpetrator has used an unaltered image.

For an altered or deepfake image of an adult to fall foul of the law, other elements must be involved. The created image must be regarded as 'grossly offensive' (contravening section 127(1) of the Communications Act 2003), and it must be proven that the pseudo-image was sent for the purpose of causing 'needless anxiety'. To prove this offence, prosecutors must establish a hostile motive towards the victim. If this type of image was sent for a joke, for example, this is not likely to contravene the act. The elements of this offence are notoriously subjective and difficult to prove.

Given this context, it is perhaps unsurprising that such acts are rarely reported, let alone investigated. Prosecutions for this type of offence are rare, despite government guidelines stipulating that this type of offence can be serious.

Regulating new cyber-crime

The regulation of technology requires the law to keep abreast of rapidly changing and highly complex trends. Telegram is only one example of the ever-growing interest in 'deepfake' images and video. It is also likely that they will become increasingly realistic.

The UK is considering legislation whereby social media platforms could face fines for facilitating such images. The government has proposed to make companies such as Telegram take more responsibility for the safety of their users and tackle harm caused by content or activity on their service. But progress has faltered, and the legislation may not be passed until 2023.

This is unfortunate. Apps which facilitate or produce fake images for general consumption are a dangerous trend which will not dissipate without considerable change to the current legal framework.

6 November 2020

Deepfake pornography: a new epidemic of violence against women

By Mila Stricevic

One of the internet's first encounters with 'deepfake' technology was a seemingly harmless viral video of Tom Cruise on social media. Despite the trivial nature of the video, even at the time serious ethical concerns were being raised about the implications of unleashing this technology into the world. Just two years later these concerns have been legitimised by the rapid circulation of deepfake pornography.

Deepfake technology allows people to generate pornographic material using only a person's face. Victims of this technology are often women and girls, whose faces are inserted into violent, graphic porn which is so realistic that it can be difficult to tell it has been computer-generated. Deepfake pornography is a freely accessible and increasingly popular avenue of violence toward women.

While it is illegal in Scotland to distribute intimate videos, images, or other content without consent under the Abusive Behaviour and Sexual Harm Act 2016, deepfake technology uses 'likeness' rather than featuring the victims themselves, making it difficult to legislate against. Furthermore, those intent on creating and distributing deepfake pornography often operate anonymously and are therefore hard to catch.

The harmful consequences of unregulated deepfake pornography are immeasurable. Victims suffer life-changing consequences including psychological distress, sexual objectification, and reputational damage. In 2021, one deepfake pornography website received over 38 million visits in eight months. It's clear this is not a hidden market.

As Megan Farokhmanesh pointed out in *Wired* magazine, much of the discussion around deepfake pornography deliberately downplays the serious harm it can cause. Whether or not the content is real makes little difference to the impact on the victim. Earlier this year, the subject came to light again, after Brandon Ewing, a streamer on Twitch, was caught with deepfake pornography featuring fellow female streamers. Among the victims, streamer QTCinderella said 'even though it's not my body, it might as well be. It was the same feeling – a violation that comes with seeing a body that's not yours being represented as yours.'

Last month, a new report from the UK's all-party parliamentary group (APPG) on commercial sexual exploitation demonstrated an inextricable link between the consumption of pornography and sexual violence against women. 'What has become apparent during the course of this inquiry is that we cannot end the epidemic of male violence against women and girls without confronting and combating the contributory role that pornography plays in fuelling sexual objectification and sexual violence.'

The fact that sexual violence in pornography carries over into our streets is distressing but it should hardly come as a surprise. Figures released in 2023 by the non-profit organisation Common Sense found that 8 in 10 teenagers who watch pornography do so for educational purposes. Of those, over 50% said they had viewed graphic porn depicting rape or people in physical distress. How can we expect young men to value respect and consent when mainstream porn epitomises violence and objectification?

Violence against women is increasing. This will continue as long as sex education (or its absence) promotes aggression, sexual violence and rape.

But the online pornography landscape is changing. The APPG has recommended that all pornography websites verify consumer age and demanded that companies ensure anyone featured in pornographic content is of legal age and consenting. Glossy policy recommendations will not protect women and girls from the distressing effects of deep fake pornography.

And deep fake technology doesn't just threaten women's safety. There are legitimate concerns that it could be used for political gain, from interfering with elections to starting wars. This technology threatens the very notion of discernible reality and truth. Deepfake content is making it virtually impossible for any media consumer, from private citizen to government official, to tell fact from fiction.

Legislation passed by the European Parliament in 2022 focused on regulating consensual deepfake content. The UK parliament has announced intentions to add the criminalisation of non-consensual deepfake pornography to the Online Safety Bill. Sentiment is simply not enough.

With more and more of our lives sacrificed to the internet, we must continue to demand action from our government to tackle the dangers of unregulated, non-consensual deepfake technology. If we don't, we are allowing our politicians to put the rights of Artificial Intelligence over those of its own citizens.

15 March 2023

www.roarnews.co.uk

Beyond shame: tackling porn addiction

Porn is nothing new, but its prevalence is. Now, some men and women from the first generation with unlimited access are switching it off. When a choice becomes a compulsion, where can people turn?

By Lucy Purdy

It's a radical experiment that has never before been attempted in history. What happens when photos and videos of every sex act imaginable can be instantly accessed by anyone, anywhere? How does this impact our brains, minds and hearts? This experiment has just become possible – and the guinea pigs are you and I.

Whether you think pornography is harmless personal entertainment, an unambiguous evil or somewhere in between, its prevalence might shock you. One of the world's biggest porn websites, Pornhub, attracted 28.5 billion visitors in 2017, around 81 million a day. (There are only 7.6 billion people in the world). Around a quarter of all internet searches are for pornographic content, and porn sites receive more regular traffic than Netflix, Amazon and Twitter combined each month.

One UK survey found that 53 per cent of 11 to 16-year-olds have seen explicit material online, and nearly all of these by the time they were 14. Laura Bates, founder of the Everyday Sexism campaign, recently warned that some schoolboys think that making girls cry during sex is normal, due to the 'misogyny and dehumanising' nature of online pornography.

Whether it's the way porn can normalise sexual aggression, degrade women (but also men), its links with sex trafficking, or the way it distorts and desensitises people to real-life sex and relationships, the $97 billion (£76 billion) industry has always attracted criticism.

> **Pornhub attracted 28.5 billion visitors in 2017, around 81 million a day. There are only 7.6 billion people in the world**

But some of those now speaking out against porn are from the very same demographic as its most avid consumers: modern men who grew up seeing porn as children and teens.

In the form of online community groups, apps, blogs, podcasts and educational videos, they are helping men and women leave porn behind and rewire their brains for what they believe is a healthier – real-life – alternative.

Pornography on the brain

The human brain has evolved to reward us for having sex by releasing dopamine at orgasm. So porn use over time can rewire the brain to 'prefer' pornography. This can happen even if the person experiences shame or disgust about it. Though medical and scientific communities disagree about whether 'porn addiction' is a genuine condition, addictive behaviour develops when someone seeks out porn in response to triggers like being bored, alone, stressed or anxious.

Some partners who find out that their loved one has been using porn feel lied to, and can experience 'betrayal trauma'. In the UK, counsellors who are trained to treat sexual addictions can be found at atsac.co.uk

Suspect that your relationship with porn is problematic? These projects could help

Fortify

App and web platform that is designed to help teens and adults overcome porn addiction.

Brainbuddy

App that offers porn-users alternatives to looking at it: from activities to inspiring videos. The brain needs to develop new pleasurable associations with technology, goes the thinking here.

Reboot Nation

Forum and online video channel offering advice for young people who believe they are addicted to pornography, have sexual dysfunction as a result and want to give porn up.

Bloom

Digital community that provides therapy and online courses for women 'who are healing from the trauma of infidelity', including the partners of some porn users.

21 January 2021

Why age verification is another flawed attempt to regulate online pornography in the UK

An article from The Conversation.

By Oliver Carter, Reader in Creative Economies, Birmingham City University

The UK government has announced that its forthcoming online safety bill will require websites that publish pornography to verify users are over 18.

Sites will need to adopt a method of age verification, such as having users provide their passport information. They will likely need to employ a third-party provider to set up and maintain these systems.

This isn't the first attempt to restrict access to online pornography in this way in Britain. The government shelved plans for a similar age verification scheme in 2019.

There's no question child safety online is critically important. But if adopted, this move will be yet another piece of legislation to add to a messy patchwork of often flawed UK laws seeking to police pornography.

I've done research on the history of pornography in Britain, and particularly its regulation. In short, this has always been a problematic area.

By the end of the 1950s, the pornography business had begun to expand. The Obscene Publications Act 1959 sought to criminalise distributors of pornography, but had the opposite effect. Its ambiguous terminology gave way to loopholes that entrepreneurs exploited, creating a thriving market for illicit goods that were sold in bookshops, via mail-order and exported to Europe in the 1960s and early 1970s.

By the end of the 1970s, there was a shift in the discourse from viewing pornography as an obscene object to questioning its impact and potential harm. A moral panic around pornography ensued, leading to a range of new laws aimed at regulating access.

For example, the Indecent Displays (Control) Act 1981 and the Local Government (miscellaneous provisions) Act 1982 sought to regulate the growth of sex shops beyond London's Soho. Their neon-lit displays were replaced by blacked out windows.

Concerns around children's access to pornography and violent material underpinned the Video Recordings Act 1984, which was deigned to regulate the new technology of home video.

In 2000, Britain appeared to liberalise its pornography laws following a review of the British Board of Film Classification R18 certificate. Hardcore pornography could legally be sold in Britain, but under strict control.

The shift of pornography to cyberspace complicated attempts at regulation further. Concerns around access to harmful pornography online led to the possession of "extreme" pornography being criminalised under the Criminal Justice and Immigration Act 2008.

If European countries such as Denmark, Netherlands and Sweden have been relatively relaxed their approach to policing pornography (Denmark was the first country to fully legalise pornography in 1969) Britain's method has been to introduce a range of messy, overlapping laws. This becomes clear when you look at the Crown Prosecution Service's advice for prosecutors to consider a list of 14 laws before deciding whether to pursue an obscenity conviction.

Perspectives from the industry

Age verification for pornography was included in the Digital Economy Act 2017. Here, authority was to be given to a government-appointed regulator to impose penalties on websites refusing to adopt age verification, such as fines or ordering internet service providers to block access.

Between 2016 and 2019 I was researching the history of Britain's pornography business and attending regular meetings of the United Kingdom Adult Performers Network.

Producers and distributors expressed concern about the impact of the Digital Economy Act 2017 on their business, fearing that age verification would dissuade customers from accessing their content. Would you want to visit a porn site if you had to put in your driver's licence details or your passport?

With pornography shifting from a physical to a digital commodity that is freely streamed by video aggregator sites such as Pornhub, small-scale producers viewed the measure as another threat to their dwindling profits.

Producers believed that age verification benefited large, powerful companies such as Mindgeek, which owns many of the popular streaming sites and production studios, and

was offering to provide age verification services to smaller operators.

Importantly, Britain's pornography producers and distributors were not opposed to age verification in theory. Indeed, they were concerned about children accessing inappropriate material. Their worry was about how this would work in practice, and the impact it would have on their business.

In the end, in 2019, the Conservative government deemed age verification for pornography websites unworkable and dropped its plans.

Now it's back on the table

Britain's renewed commitment to age restriction follows similar moves in France and Germany.

Under the online safety bill, power would be afforded to the UK's communications regulator Ofcom, making it responsible for determining how websites are dealt with if they fail to verify users' age. Social platforms containing pornographic content, like Reddit and Twitter, may not be exempt.

Privacy concerns remain, particularly around the potential for leaked data that identifies personal sexual interests.

We will now wait and see whether the government's plans for age verification will succeed. But history shows that Britain's pornography laws have never been fit for purpose. Producers and audiences have always found loopholes to circumvent controls. Some young, tech-savvy users are likely to do the same with this law.

10 February 2022

Brits strongly support porn age-verification checks

Eight in ten Britons believe pornography websites should ensure all users are over the age of 18, new polling has revealed.

Of the 1148 adults surveyed by PeoplePolling for GB News, 78 per cent backed the use of age-verification checks to prevent children from gaining access to online pornography. Only 5 per cent disagreed with the proposal.

Lord Bethell is seeking to amend the Government's Online Safety Bill in order to force pornography websites to start verifying the age of users within six months of the legislation becoming law.

Political spectrum

The majority of Conservative voters (84 per cent), Labour voters (80 per cent), and Liberal Democrat voters (80 per cent) agreed that more should be done to protect children from online pornography.

The survey also demonstrated strong support among young adults for pornography websites to have age verification systems, with nearly six in ten (59 per cent) 18 to 24-year-olds in favour of the idea.

Speaking to GB News, politics Professor Matthew Goodwin said the survey demonstrated widespread public support for Lord Bethell's amendment.

I've never seen numbers like this in a poll really before, we've got about 78 per cent of the country expressing support for having these checks for children ensuring they can't access pornography online. – Professor Matthew Goodwin

Loopholes

Age verification checks were approved under the Digital Economy Act 2017, but plans to implement them were abandoned in October 2019.

Lord Bethell argues that the current definition of age verification in the Online Safety Bill is not strong enough, and the legislation's measures could create loopholes for websites to claim it would be too difficult to enforce checks.

24 February 2023

Beyond age verification: towards a more nuanced understanding of young people's experiences of pornography

By Emily Setty and Ellen Harris

The government has recently announced that it is finally knocking on the head the perhaps well-intentioned but inevitably ill-conceived idea for an age verification system for online pornography. Under the law, porn websites would have had to establish that UK-based visitors to the sites are over the age of 18. Aside from well-documented privacy concerns, the ease of users circumventing such requirements through the use of Virtual Private Networks (VPNs) and debates over what constitutes 'sexually explicit' material online, there is a question here about the stated aim of the policy to 'protect' children and young people from sexual content deemed harmful to them and the role of pornography in their broader sexual lives, development and self-concepts.

Given that evidence suggests that younger teenagers tend to first encounter online pornography 'accidentally' (e.g. via a 'pop-up'), there may be some rationale to a system designed to block 'sexually explicit' material until a user has verified their age. Perspectives and experiences seem, however, to become more multifaceted and nuanced as young people get older. Older teenagers disclose various motivations for accessing pornography and their attitudes and experiences are gendered in that older boys are seemingly more likely to deliberately access pornography and to perceive it positively. The irrelevance of the proposed age verification system in light of older young people's willingness and ability to circumvent attempts to monitor and block their access to online content (both sexual and non-sexual) cannot be denied.

The implications of pornography for young people may be complex and contradictory. It has the potential to challenge 'repression and restrictive sexual' norms and aid in the development of sexual knowledge, self-efficacy and self-esteem but also to reflect and reinforce gender and sexual inequalities and stereotypes. There is, therefore, a need to understand what young people are viewing and how they are engaging with it. Efforts to block their access to pornography will not diminish the need for these open and honest conversations, however awkward and challenging they may be both for young people and adults.

In research with teenagers, Emily Setty, Lecturer in Criminology at the University of Surrey, found that interventions and education that are negative in tone and seek only highlight the 'dangers' of pornography are unlikely to suffice. This research revealed that pornography is part of young people's broader sexual and relational cultures; significant is not just what they are watching but how they are engaging with it and how it relates and contributes to their sexual self-concepts. As found in other research, young people tended to normalise teenage boys' use of pornography and the boys were often resistant to attempts to problematise and curtail their access to pornography. For some boys, uncritical celebration of pornography was part of masculine participation within male peer groups. The girls, meanwhile, often constructed pornography as 'weird', 'shameful' and 'anti-feminist' for them to watch, but also threatening to them in terms of the objectified and unrealistic depictions of women's appearance and sexuality, and the risk that boys may 'prefer' pornography to 'real-life' sex and may 'betray' them by continuing to watch pornography when in relationships.

The boys' perspectives were complex, however, with some experiencing feelings of shame and self-doubt connected to their use of pornography. The materiality of pornography – in terms of the depiction of male appearance and sexual performance – was disconcerting to some of them. Some also described feeling desensitised to ever-more extreme pornography characterised by pain and degradation. While some felt this means that pornography is just a harmless fantasy and perfectly 'healthy' so long as they can still enjoy 'real-life' sex, others questioned the ethics of the industry and described feeling ashamed by what they find arousing and confused about what girls find pleasurable.

Young people are, it seems, critically engaging with pornography. They tussle with what is 'normal' and 'acceptable' and the nature of pleasure, desire and arousal. They were, however, quite individualistic in their narratives. They tended not to connect their feelings of confusion and ambivalence to broader gender and sexual inequalities and stereotypes. Some boys, for example, 'suspected' that girls are more sexual and watch pornography more than they let on; they seemed to eroticise this 'secret sexuality', however, and did not reflect on why girls may feel compelled to construct themselves as uninterested in pornography. The girls, meanwhile, often harnessed discourses of 'feminism' and 'empowerment' in their opposition to pornography, but their taken-for-granted beliefs that women are not 'visually-stimulated' and are more interested in emotion and relationships than embodied sexual pleasure reflected and reinforced the gender double standards within their broader relational and sexual cultures.

Ellen Harris, PhD Researcher at the University of Surrey, intends for her research to shed further light on girls' and young women's perspectives on pornography. While there is increasing recognition that boys' perspectives are complex, Ellen's research will explore what underlies the socially-approved narrative that girls don't watch pornography. Rather than accepting that girls are inherently uninterested in (albeit potentially threatened by) pornography, Ellen is interested in why girls produce these narratives. Her research aims to explore and understand their perspectives and the role pornography plays in their sexual and relational lives. She hopes for the findings to reveal the diversity and complexity of girls' experiences, as well as inform an educational and policy context which often assumes that pornography viewers are heterosexual boys whose use of porn is problematic for girls.

With Sex and Relationships Education to soon become mandatory in most schools in England, the time is ripe for considering how pornography could represent a resource for bringing to life the complexities around sex, relationships, gender and sexuality. These issues are not just pertinent to young people; pornography is designed by and – ostensibly – intended for adults, and there is a need for openness about what the norms and values contained within pornography reveal about society more broadly as well as the implications for young people's sexual development and learning. Rather than problematising young people's perspectives, we should reflect on what we are modelling and the value systems that shape how we engage with young people. Neither blocking nor simply just 'more education' is, therefore, enough; targeted interventions and education should be more meaningful and youth-centred, but we should also acknowledge what young people are learning and experiencing within their situated cultures more broadly, of which adults may play a part.

8 November 2019

Further Reading/ Useful Websites

Useful Websites

www.childrenscommissioner.gov.uk

www.brook.org.uk

www.cease.org.uk

www.christian.org.uk

www.ditchthelabel.org

www.fightthenewdrug.org

www.ifstudies.org

www.independent.co.uk

www.lse.ac.uk

www.positive.news

www.realclearscience.com

www.roarnews.co.uk

www.socialistworker.co.uk

www.stuartmillersolicitors.co.uk

www.surrey.ac.uk

www.theconversation.com

www.theguardian.com

www.welldoing.org

www.yougov.co.uk

Where can I find help?

Below are some telephone numbers, email addresses and websites of agencies or charities that can offer support or advice if you, or someone you know, needs it.

Childline
Helpline: 0800 1111
Website: www.childline.org.uk

CEOP
If you have experienced online sexual abuse or you're worried this is happening to someone you know you can report it online
Website: www.ceop.police.uk

Shout
Provides 24/7 urgent mental health support
text SHOUT to 85258
Website: www.giveusashout.org

Revenge Porn Helpline
Helpline: 0345 6000 459
Email: help@revengepornhelpline.org.uk
Website: www.revengepornhelpline.org.uk

Further Reading

Page 1: You can view the original article from Brook at www.brook.org.uk/your-life/porn/

Glossary

Automatic porn filters

Some people feel that automatic porn filters are needed in order to protect people, particularly children, from viewing disturbing pornographic images online. The idea is that, on purchasing a new PC or Internet service, adults would be forced to choose which types of content they wanted to be accessed on their computer. This would mean that any site categorised as inappropriate – sites containing porn, suicide, self-harm, etc. – would be blocked. There is concern, however, that this could result in genuine websites being blocked unfairly, for example medical or self-help sites.

Censorship

When there are restrictions on what people can see or hear and on the information they are allowed to access, this is called censorship. By censoring something, an individual, publication or Government is preventing the whole truth from coming out or stopping something from being heard or seen at all. Items may also be censored or restricted to protect vulnerable people such as children, and to prevent public offence.

Child Sexual Exploitation (CSE)

Using or exploiting a child for sexual purposes. This often goes hand-in-hand with the grooming process and can involve offering the child money, gifts, cigarettes or alcohol in return for sexual favours. CSE can lead to child trafficking and prostitution.

Classifications

Also called age ratings. Films in cinemas and on DVD, as well as computer games, must carry a classification indicating a minimum age at which the material should be watched or played. It is a criminal offence for a retailer to supply an age-restricted DVD or game to someone below the required age.

Coercive sex acts

Sexual activity which involves pressure or manipulation (in pornography this may be presented as real or simulated) and a persistent attempt to have sexual contact with someone who has already refused.

Degrading sex acts

Sexual acts which are intended to cause humiliation, shame or emotional distress

Objectify/Objectification

To turn something into an object in relation to sight, touch or another physical sense. To 'objectify' a person means to turn them into an object, meaning that they do not possess the same human rights as another individual. The person objectified is usually dominated by another person, or group of people.

Online harms

Content or activity that can cause harm to internet users, particularly children and vulnerable people. These behaviours can harm people either emotionally or physically

Physically aggressive sex acts

Sexual acts which carry a reasonable risk of physical harm, regardless of the perpetrator's intent and the recipient's response.

Pornification

Very similar to sexualisation, the term pornification refers to the acceptance of sexualisation in our culture.

Pornography

Images or videos that explicitly portray sexual activity.

Rape

Forcing someone to engage in sexual intercourse against their will. Force is not necessarily physical, it could also be emotional or psychological.

Rape culture

An environment or culture that normalises sexual violence, trivialises sexual assault and tolerates sexual harassment against (mostly) women. Rape culture often blames and shames victims while excusing the perpetrator.

Revenge porn

Revenge porn refers to distributing or making public explicit images or videos of a former partner.

Sex trafficking

Transporting people from one area to another in order to force them to work in the sex trade – usually as prostitutes, but they could be forced into the porn industry also. Sex trafficking does not just occur between countries, it also happens within the UK and is closely linked to child sexual exploitation and grooming.

Sexual abuse

Sexual abuse occurs when a victim is forced into a sexual act against their will, through violence or intimidation. This can include rape. Sexual abuse is always a crime, no matter what the relationship is between the victim and perpetrator.

Sexualise/Sexualisation

To give someone or something sexual characteristics and associations. This refers to the idea that sex has become much more visible in culture and media today. Premature sexualisation of children involves exposure to sexual images and ideas at an age when they are emotionally unable to process such information. Implications include children having sex at a younger age, engaging in activities such as sexting, an increased likelihood of their being groomed; and it has been linked to hypermasculine behaviour in boys and young men.

Sexual violence

Any sexual act which may be considered as degrading, physically aggressive or coercive.

Index

A
accidental viewing 1, 5, 10, 15, 40
addiction 23, 24–25, 37
age
    and first exposure to porn 14–15
    and watching porn 16, 18–19
age verification 5, 9, 38–39, 40
attitudes to sex 20

B
behaviour, effect on 3, 6, 11, 12 *see also*
  addiction
body image 11, 16–17, 22, 27
boys' perspectives on porn 40–41

C
capitalism 7–8
child pornography 4, 28
child protection 28–29, 34–35
coercion 12, 30–31
commodification of sex 7–8, 31
consent 2, 27
Covid-19 28

D
deepfake images 34–36

E
Eilish, Billie 9
emotional effects 9, 16–17, 22–23
ethical porn 3, 8, 31
expectations of real-life sex 2–3, 7–8,
  10–11, 21, 27
extreme pornography 4–5

F
frequency of watching 16, 18–19, 22

G
gender
    and pleasure 2, 12
    and watching porn 16, 18–19
girls' perspectives on porn 40–41
grooming, online 29

H
help, getting 3, 32, 33, 37

I
image manipulation 34–36
indecent images 5, 28–29, 32, 34–36

K
Kalemba, Rose 30

L
laws, UK 4–5, 6, 32–33, 34–35, 38–39
  see also age verification
loneliness 16–17, 22–23

M
men 16–17, 18–19, 21, 40–41
mental health 16–17, 22–23, 24–25

O
OnlyFans 28–29

P
parents, advice for 6, 29
pleasure, gender and 2, 12
porn industry 7, 24, 30–31, 38
Porn Law (Digital Economy Act 2017) 5
Pornhub 30, 37
pressure to watch porn 1, 11
problematic use of porn 23, 24–25, 37

R
rape culture 26–27
relationship and sex education (RSE) 13
relationships, effect on 9, 12, 23
revenge porn 32–33, 35

S
safety, online 28–29
satisfaction with sex lives 17, 21
self esteem 16, 21, 22–23
sentences, criminal 4, 5, 32
sex education 9, 11, 13, 20
sexual harassment 12, 26

T
Telegram 34–35
trafficking, human 30–31
types of porn 2

U
underage viewing of porn 14–15
unhealthy use of porn 3
user-generated content 28–29

V
viewing porn, routes to 10, 15

W
women
    girls' perspectives on porn 40–41
    oppression of 7–8
    violence against 7, 12, 30–31, 36

Y
young people
    exposure to porn 9, 10, 14–15
    mental health 25
    views on porn 6, 40–41